242 M978s
The spirit of Christmas

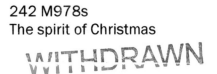

The Spirit of Christmas

Also by Cecil Murphey and Marley Gibson

Christmas Miracles

The Spirit of Christmas

Cecil Murphey *and* Marley Gibson

Foreword by *Debbie Macomber*

St. Martin's Press ⚑ New York

Grateful acknowledgment is made for permission to reprint the following: Brenda Poinsett, "Confession of the Christmas Damper," in *Can Martha Have a Mary Christmas?* in a slightly different form (Birmingham, AL: New Hope Publishers, 2005), 99–104. Used by permission.

www.stmartins.com

All biblical quotations are from the
New Living Translation (NLT).

LIBRARY OF CONGRESS
CATALOGING-IN-PUBLICATION DATA

Murphey, Cecil.
  The Spirit of Christmas / Cecil Murphey and Marley Gibson; with a foreword by Debbie Macomber.—1st ed.
       p. cm.
   ISBN 978-0-312-64501-4
  1. Christmas stories, American. 2. Christmas—Anecdotes. I. Gibson, Marley. II. Title.
   PN6071.C6M76 2011
   813'.0108334—dc23

                                   2011025837

10 9 8 7 6 5 4 3 2

Contents

Acknowledgments

Special thanks to:

- Our agent, Deidre Knight, The Knight Agency
- Rose Hilliard, our editor,
- and Cec's assistant, Twila Belk.

All three of them helped to make this book possible.

Foreword

by Debbie Macomber

You're going to love this book. It won't matter if you picked it up because you're looking for a way to get into the Christmas spirit or because you simply love the holiday season. The minute you start reading the first story, you'll find yourself unable to put the book down. I devoured every word, every story, flipping the pages, wanting more. I laughed, I cried, I poked my husband and read whole paragraphs to him.

Each and every story plows a path directly to your heart. If your family or friends complain that they just can't get into the spirit of Christmas, hand them this book. If you hear a modern-day Scrooge lamenting all the work and effort associated with Christmas, hand him—or her—this book. Trust me, they will thank you.

I read it in March, a full nine months before Christmas. By the time I turned the last page, I was ready to drag out my decorations, trim the tree, and bring out my Nativity set.

You might be saying: *Another* book about Christmas? Really? What more can people say about the most wonderful time of the year? Quite a lot, actually. True, it's a great occasion for some of us. For others it's nothing but stress, demands, family drama, and overextending our credit limits.

Whichever group you belong to, Christmas lovers, complainers, or somewhere in between, this is a book worth reading. And it's *especially* worth reading if you're a member of the down-on-Christmas group.

If, like many of us, you have memories of being alone and broke at Christmas, you'll definitely relate to Cecil Murphey's story about a surprise dinner invitation that meant the world to him and his young wife. It came from a college professor who, in giving, received the greatest gift.

Have you ever been caught in a long line at the post office? It's the worst. Traffic jams in the parking lot, hauling in packages only to discover a line that stretches out the door. That's what confronted Wayne Scheer. And yet he walked away uplifted with a smile on his face. Now *that's* the Christmas spirit, and you'll feel it all the way to your heart just as Wayne did when you read his touching story.

Jean Matthew Hall writes about the Christmas when there was absolutely no money. Not even for food. Dinners consisted of cooked oatmeal or frozen pizza. Then an unexpected delivery was made, showing us yet again that God knows our needs even before we can tell Him. Oh, there was ice cream and orange juice and turkey—an entire smorgasbord of the very best for this young family.

These are stories that will linger in your mind. Stories that remind us that Christmas isn't just a time to give and receive gifts. It's a season of love and appreciation for the gifts God has already given us. A reminder of how blessed we are with or without the material trappings of the season. These stories tell us that the poorest Christmases are often the richest ones in our memories.

There are tales of special gifts given in love by parents who sacrificed to make sure their children received that long-anticipated toy. Stories that point us to the realization that our heavenly Father chose to express His love for us through the gift of His only son. The personal accounts in this book help us understand that joy comes not from receiving but from giving of ourselves to others.

One of my favorites is Twila Belk's story about a family opening their home and hearts to a homeless family. They were blessed with a big house but no furniture—empty rooms soon filled with wall-to-wall mattresses. The Belks discovered that it was possible to be grateful for the *lack* of material goods and their stained, needing-to-be-replaced carpet. You'll enjoy reading how these two families came together to create a meaningful Christmas neither will forget.

Stories about Christmas usually feature children's wishes, but Chris Griffin tells of a wish his elderly mother made, a wish God chose to grant. It involved a fire truck driving through their neighborhood, carrying a Santa who tossed out candy to local children. This was one very special moment that allowed a woman close to the end of her life to see Him at work. The fact that God granted her wish proves that He is indeed with us and hears even the smallest of requests. Small to some, but huge to others.

While all the stories will inspire and encourage, the ones that depict Christmas miracles stirred my emotions most, such as Ada Brownell's story of driving through a blizzard to reach her daughter, Carolyn, on Christmas Day. Carolyn was dying of cancer and her parents wanted nothing more than to spend the holidays with her. Their journey through impossible conditions had me reaching for the tissue box. Yet despite the sadness, there was joy in the gift of this last Christmas with their daughter. It was truly a miracle of love.

These are personal accounts that would seem beyond imagination if they weren't true. The pages of this book are filled with stories of hope, love, sacrifice, and joy, stories that will bring you the spirit of Christmas.

Like I said, you're going to love this book!

The Spirit of
Christmas

1. Alone and Broke at Christmas

Cecil Murphey

I CHOSE TO DO MY FIRST YEAR OF COLLEGE AT A SMALL school in southern Texas—sixteen hundred miles from home. Shirley was pregnant with our first child and had complications with her pregnancy. That meant we were unable to travel back to the Chicago area for the Christmas holidays. Even if she had been able to travel, we didn't have the money.

I went to school on veteran's benefits. By watching our finances closely, we survived. We regularly ate Kraft's macaroni-and-cheese mixes, bought hurt cans and marked-down vegetables at the supermarket. Neither of us considered it a sacrifice. In many ways, it was an adventure.

Christmas season began on Tuesday and most of the afternoon the campus was a plethora of people rushing from place to place and cars driving out of the campus. The last students left early Wednesday morning. By Thursday, two days before Christmas, the classrooms were empty. They closed the library and locked the student dorms. No one would return for ten days. In the married couples' dorm we were the only ones still on campus. We didn't have a telephone and it was long before computers, so we depended on the postal service for connecting with our families.

I had checked out all the books from the library that I thought

I might want during the holiday period. I looked forward to the opportunity to study without pressure.

On Christmas Eve, Shirley and I had a meal that was a mixture of a dented can of corn and an even more dented can of chili. Someone had given us a box of candles that had been "delicately used," as the person said. Shirley had embroidered my initials on six new handkerchiefs. I had bought her a small bottle of cologne.

The church where we worshipped had a Christmas Eve service and we attended. Normally the church was full, but that night not more than thirty people came to the special service.

Christmas morning would be like any other day except we would have a nicer meal—meat loaf and baked sweet potatoes, food not normally on our diet.

About nine thirty, someone knocked on the door of our two-room apartment. I was shocked that anyone else was on campus. When I answered the door, the man smiled at me. We hadn't met, but I knew his last name was Willard. He was one of the instructors at the college.

"I heard you two were here for the holidays," he said.

"That's right." I invited him into our kitchen and to one of the four chairs we owned. I offered him a cup of coffee.

"No thanks," he said. When he came into the room, he had a strange way of walking, almost as if he swayed from one foot to the other.

"I don't want to stay," Mr. Willard said. "I'm a bachelor and I want to take you two out for Christmas dinner."

Shirley could hear us from the bedroom, where she had been lying down. She came into the room and grinned at me as I said, "We'd like that very much."

"I came early because I didn't know if you'd be preparing a big meal or had other plans to visit someone or—"

I laughed. "We have no plans." I would have countered with an invitation to share our Christmas meal, but two small sweet potatoes wouldn't be enough for three people.

"How about one o'clock? Is that all right?" After we nodded, he said, "I'll come by and pick you up."

He was five minutes early and we were ready. He took us to a fine Chinese restaurant. "They're about the only ones open today," he said.

I felt genuinely touched that he would take us out for Christmas dinner. We talked and slowly he told us about himself. He was a vet and had lost both legs in combat, which explained the strange way he walked. He shared a sad story about the woman he loved. She couldn't stand to look at his legless body and broke off their engagement. "It hurt and I loved her," he said, "but it's better that she left before we married."

For almost two hours we sat by the window and talked. I won't say it was the best Christmas I ever had, but it was a special one.

When we reached our apartment, Shirley was nauseated and hurried inside. I sat in the car and talked with Mr. Willard for a few minutes.

"Thank you," he said to me. "It means so much that you would spend part of your Christmas with me."

I invited him to come inside, but he declined. As I walked into the building, I kept hearing his words inside my head. He had made Christmas Day special for us and yet he thanked us.

A few days later I again answered the knock on our door. Mr. Willard was there, this time in his wheelchair and without his artificial legs. One of his army friends had contacted him and they were going to West Texas for New Year's.

I thanked him again for our Christmas dinner, and he held out his hand to shake mine. As I leaned down toward him, he embraced me and whispered, "You two made this a special Christmas. I was so depressed, I wondered if life was worth living."

I stared at him and felt the moisture in my eyes. I don't remember the words between us, but I do remember he pulled me down to his level and embraced me. He released me, backed up his wheelchair, and left.

I never had Mr. Willard as an instructor and I never saw him again. The following year I transferred to the Chicago area. I can't even remember his first name. What I do remember is how special he made Christmas for a young, impoverished couple. And to make it even more wonderful, he thanked *us*.

I've learned many lessons about Christmas, but this is one I treasure. He gave to us and yet he seemed to get more pleasure out of the giving than we did out of the receiving. That truly is the Christmas spirit, isn't it?

2. That Chaotic Christmas

Marley Gibson

"CHRISTMAS IS CANCELED," MY MOTHER SAID STERNLY, HER eyes moist with tears. Only two months earlier she had lost her beloved father to heart disease.

"You can't cancel Christmas," I said.

"Yes, I can. Daddy is no longer with us and it doesn't matter to me this year."

That shocked me because I'd often thought of my mother as the Queen of Christmastime. She was a church organist, taught carols to the kids, and led the choir in seasonal musicals. She played for her church with such fervor I sometimes wondered if the angels were channeling their choruses through her.

Christmas canceled?

It wasn't that I was upset about not having presents or toys. I was eighteen, a freshman in college, and I didn't need those material items. What I wanted was the Christmas tree put up the way my mother did it every year with the ornaments organized exactly right. What I needed was the smell of Christmas turkey as we gathered around the dining room table with many delicious, homemade side dishes. What I yearned for was to hear my mother sit at our piano in the living room and sing about the birth of Christ, the ultimate present God gave to the world that brings us peace, love, and joy all through the year.

Christmas canceled?

"Not if I have anything to say about it," my sister, Jennifer, said on the phone. "If Mom won't put up the tree, we'll do it."

"I'll help, too!" my brother, Jeff, yelled.

"I'll help, as well," Dad told me. "But your mother isn't going to be happy about this."

We even got our grandmother in on the plans, knowing she wouldn't want to be alone on Christmas Day without Granddaddy.

The decision was made: We *would* have Christmas.

For me, it felt like a long December, finishing finals at college and coming home to find the house just as it was the rest of the year: No tree. No wreath. No candles. No crèche. Even my cat, Smokey, walked around twitching his nose and tail as if knowing something wasn't right.

My brother, Jeff, arrived, followed by my sister, Jennifer. She had driven from New Jersey to Alabama with her two cats, Jo and Natalie. We were prepared for a full-frontal, all-family-members Christmas assault on my mother.

While she was out one afternoon, Jennifer, Jeff, and I began to decorate the house. We put the artificial tree together, hung the lights, strung the tinsel, and placed the ornaments in the best way we could to make it look like Mom had done it. I carefully unwrapped each hand-painted item of the crèche and set Mary, Joseph, the wise men, camel, sheep, angel, and, finally, baby Jesus on top of the piano among holly leaves and berries.

Jennifer decorated the mantel with pinecones, Christmas cards, and candles. Jeff put Mom's wreath on the front door and placed a spotlight in the lawn to highlight it. We were ready to face Mom.

Minutes later, her car pulled up and we waited.

She walked inside, put down her purse, and said nothing. The former Queen of Christmastime went into her room.

While our family drama was going on, a feud had begun. Smokey hadn't liked having two other creatures invade his space. Jo and Natalie slept in his favorite spots, ate his food, and ganged up on him. He was definitely not full of the Christmas spirit.

We kids bought the turkey and were going to cook it Christmas Day to the best of our ability. It wouldn't be Mom's cooking, but we were going to have our Christmas feast.

Christmas Eve, Mom went to church while Jennifer and Jeff went to visit a friend. Dad and I cooked breakfast food for our dinner. As we quietly ate our pancakes and bacon, a horrid screech, like a mountain lion calling out, filled the room.

"Was that the cats?" I asked.

Dad just raised an eyebrow, shrugged, and went back to eating.

Seconds later a cacophony of sounds mixed together as the animals rushed down the stairs. Meows, howls, and hissing filled the house. Apparently Smokey had had enough and was defending his territory from the two females who'd been torturing him the past few days. All of them ran around the house, through the living room, and under the dining room table.

Three flashes of black fur were a blur as Dad and I tried to separate them. Jo bolted underneath the Christmas tree, followed by Natalie. Smokey pursued. The jumbled mess of cat-ness disappeared under the green branches lit with colorful lights.

As the catfight continued, the tree began to shake. The ornaments clanged and shivered. Dad and I didn't know what to do, so we watched. Just then the tree started to shake and tip forward.

Dad and I did our best to catch it, but the tree hit the living room floor with a loud crack.

Even though Mom wasn't in her regular Christmas frame of mind, one thing I knew was that she would freak out seeing the tree and her ornaments scattered across the floor. Dad and I only had a few minutes before she'd come home from church.

Without Jennifer and Jeff there to help—Jeff knew how to set up the tree just like Mom—Dad and I did our best to return the tree to normal. Dad tightened the trunk in the base and I toiled over returning the lights and garland to some semblance of normalcy. It took quite an effort on our part, but we succeeded in righting the tree and straightening it minutes before the front door opened.

Mom stared at Dad and me in the living room trying to act as if nothing had happened. We probably had discomfort written on our faces.

"Those damn cats knocked down the Christmas tree, didn't they?" Mom said.

"How did you know?" I asked.

"Because it's crooked and everything's a mess."

Dad shrugged and looked at me. "We tried."

I started laughing. Hard. I couldn't help it.

And so did Mom. It was the first time we'd heard her laughter in a couple of months—in fact, not since Granddaddy's death.

Finally, she gazed around the living room and took in that we'd decorated for her. Tears filled her eyes and she went over and sat at the piano. She ran her hand gently over the figurines of the crèche and paused over the baby Jesus.

That's when the spirit of Christmas refilled my mother's broken heart and she stretched her fingers out onto the ivory keys. She began to play and sing "Joy to the World."

Yes, there was joy to the world. Our family was together that Christmas and we would celebrate the most joyous day of the year together. We would miss not having Granddaddy with us, but he was in heaven with Jesus—where he'd always wanted to be. And that only added to our Christmas spirit.

Christmas had been uncanceled.

While Mother continued to sing, I went upstairs to seek out the culprits of our Christmas chaos. There they were. Smokey, Jo, and Natalie were all curled up on *my bed* in one large kitty ball.

I laughed and shook my head. Indeed, there was joy in the world.

3. A Tuna Christmas

Dan Piper

IN THE WINTER OF 1988, THE YOUNG PEOPLE DECIDED THAT rather than giving gifts to one another, we would bring food items for the poor in our community. As the kids entered the party they put food items on a large table labeled "Gifts for the King." We reasoned that Christmas is His birthday, so we have a birthday party for Him. We conclude each party by singing "Happy Birthday" to Jesus.

I served as the Minister of Youth and Education at South Park Church. Our Youth Council planned our annual "Birthday Party for Jesus" in the church's Fellowship Hall. The "Birthday Party for Jesus" was our version of a Christmas party celebrated as a birthday party complete with birthday cake, candles, and gifts.

Near the party's end, we turned off the lights, lit the birthday candles, and sang "Happy Birthday" to Jesus.

After the party we planned to use the church vans and deliver the food to already-identified families in need. We put the food items into grocery bags and loaded the food onto the waiting vans. Within minutes, the windows of the vans were fogged with the breath of teens as they sang carols and generally made happy noise.

Our first stop was a small two-room house where thirteen people lived. We carried our bags of food inside and they graciously received us. The residents spoke little English, but there was much bowing and smiling. Words weren't needed to know their sincere appreciation.

After shaking hands and wishing them a blessed Christmas, we walked back to our waiting vans for our second and final stop of the evening. Inside the van the tone was now somewhat more subdued, quieter, more reflective, but still upbeat.

We looked carefully at each house to find our correct address. Dusk isn't easy on the eyes, but we finally found the place and pulled into the driveway. Just then, the front door of the modest home opened and several barefoot children leaped off the porch and ran up to the van before the church kids could even get out.

Apparently the children wanted to help us carry their gifts inside. Overwhelmed by their excitement, we handed them the smaller bags. The children were like six small stair steps ranging from age four to ten. Because they were so small, each could carry only a tiny load. It disturbed me to see their bare feet on the cold ground. But they didn't seem to be bothered.

To our surprise, no adults waited inside the house.

"Is your mommy or daddy at home?" I asked.

"No, sir," the youngest said, and smiled sweetly. "They're working."

"Can we just put these gifts down on the kitchen table?"

"Oh yes!" All six of them lined up around the table. Six skinny, shoeless waifs stood there looking as if we had just delivered a million dollars to their kitchen table.

We had only delivered green beans, hominy, corn, Spam, or anything else some church kid's mom took from her pantry.

It didn't seem like much when our young people brought it to the party. But as I thought of those kids' joy, it seemed like the making of a sumptuous feast.

One girl climbed up on a well-worn dinette chair and peered into the opening of the Kroger sack. As she gazed over the brown bag's edge her little impish face lit up as if she beheld glory. Reaching down gently, with great reverence, she withdrew one can of Bumble Bee tuna.

Clutching it to her breast, she looked heavenward and exclaimed, "Tuna fish, I love tuna fish!"

That was such a powerful moment that none of us said anything. She was excited over a can of tuna—as if it were a precious treasure. Fighting with my own emotions, I said softly, "Maybe your mom will fix it for you tonight."

"Oh, I hope so!" she said, and giggled. Still clutching her can of tuna, she climbed down from her chair and hugged each of us.

The church kids mustered a faint, "Merry Christmas," and went out into the cool December evening. The vision of those six barefoot children waving from the front porch as we walked to the waiting church van still remains in my memory. And the sight of a little girl with one hand sweetly waving and the other clutching her precious tuna stays with me even today.

For several minutes none of us said anything, as if each of us was lost in our own thoughts. Perhaps the church kids were praying for those kids. Maybe they were telling God how grateful they were for His bountiful blessings in their own lives. Were they remembering all the times that they had turned up their noses at food lovingly prepared? Quite possibly a few tears gently flowed down a cheek or two. I don't know because, although I was driving, I was misty-eyed and faced forward so no one could see my face.

I'm amazed at how often I'm reminded of the face of that little girl clutching her can of Bumble Bee tuna as if it were a priceless jewel. Many times I asked, "Should it take a holiday to remind us that there are folks who are in need three hundred and sixty-five days a year?" To remind me, I keep a can of tuna on a bookshelf in my office.

And I hope that precious little girl's mom prepared that tuna for her that night as we celebrated the birth of Jesus.

A can of tuna for Christmas seems like so little, but to the child it seemed like so much. I sometimes think that's how it was with God's invention of Christmas. Some saw a babe and scoffed; others saw a Savior and rejoiced. It's all in the perceived value, isn't it?

4. Christmas at the Post Office

Wayne Scheer

I AGREED TO TAKE CHRISTMAS PRESENTS TO THE POST OF-fice to mail them. I knew I made a mistake as soon as I pulled into the parking lot. Usually, half a dozen cars are parked near the entrance, with a few others scattered about. This time, the lot was full and I had to pull into the parking lot of a bank across the street. I took a deep breath and prepared myself for the true sacrifice of the season—crowds with nasty tempers.

A few steps into the overheated building and I was in line. A woman with a young child came immediately behind me, and a middle-aged man stood behind her. Within minutes, the queue extended outside the building. Feeling pleased with myself for arriving just in time, I tried not to notice the sea of people holding their packages like life preservers.

To my surprise, I couldn't complain about the postal workers. Looking at the long counter where they weighed packages and assessed postage, I didn't see a single "This station closed" sign. Five people—three men and two women—worked at an efficient pace. The line moved slowly, but at least it moved. Each time I took a full step forward, I felt a wave of satisfaction.

The euphoria didn't last. My packages grew heavy and the room felt stuffy. A man in front of me complained loudly on his cell phone about wasting his valuable time. A woman kept pulling up the sleeve of her coat to check her watch, as if that would speed things up.

Behind me, a young boy whined, "I'm bored."

"So am I," his mother said. "Nothing we can do about it."

I turned toward her and nodded. She appeared uncomfortable with the approval of a stranger and grabbed her son's hand. I took the hint and stared straight ahead.

Christmas music blared over the general grumbling of the masses. A man said loudly, "If I hear Brenda Lee singing 'Rockin' Around the Christmas Tree,' I'm converting to Buddhism and moving to Tibet."

An elderly Chinese couple about halfway up the line, both of whom were barely five feet tall, stood in expressionless silence, as if to say, "I've seen much worse." Something about their rumpled clothing and deeply wrinkled faces calmed me.

The line continued to move slowly. I watched one of the postal workers, a large African-American woman, in what seemed like a heated exchange with a young man with a shaven head. I had no idea what the argument was about, but it appeared to me that the woman had lost her patience and the phrase "going postal" flashed through my mind. The man finally left, showing no evidence of Christmas cheer. The next person took his place, and I moved forward one more step.

The elderly couple drew my attention again. The man had repositioned his packages under his arms to free his hands. He turned toward his wife and waved his fingers as if conducting an orchestra. Just then I realized he was using sign language to communicate with her. I watched them make deaf speech utterances to each other. The man nodded, took one of the packages from the woman, and they returned to their stoicism.

I felt humbled, more willing to accept my place in line. I imagined them alone in an alien, silent world. I couldn't tell if either of them could speak or even if they spoke English, but it didn't seem to matter. I hoped their packages were marked clearly so they'd have no problem when they finally reached the counter.

I moved forward a few steps. The clock on the wall showed I had been there twenty minutes; it seemed much longer. Crepe paper and tinsel decorated the walls and the counter, but nothing else appeared festive. I watched the Chinese couple in their profound silence as they moved up next in line.

I had a new worry. I hoped I didn't get the large black woman who worked with a scowl and no-nonsense efficiency. That had nothing to do with her race. The other postal workers, black and white, appeared friendly enough and, to my mind, would show more patience.

The woman, whose frown seemed deeply ingrained, yelled, "Next!" and the elderly couple, barely able to reach over the counter, unloaded their packages. The man tried to say something to the woman, but between his sign language and his accent communication appeared impossible.

The female clerk stared at him and his wife, who pointed to her own lips and shook her head. I wanted to reach out to the couple and protect them from what I feared would follow.

As if in a Christmas movie directed by Frank Capra, the postal worker's grimace magically transformed to an open-faced grin and her fingers fluttered in rapid motion. The three of them began signing excitedly. The woman spoke aloud slowly as she signed, and I figured out that the couple wanted to mail presents to their grandchildren who lived in London.

While the postal worker weighed the packages, the man took pictures from his wallet to show her. Remarkably, no one complained as the postal clerk stopped to view each picture and nod approvingly. The elderly man even turned to a woman nearby to show his photos.

When he paid for the postage, he took out an additional bill—it looked like a twenty—and handed it to the woman behind the counter. "You. Christmas."

"No," she said, shaking her head emphatically and overarticulating her words as she signed. "But there is one thing I want."

She came from behind the counter and held out her arms. The woman was even larger than I had imagined, towering over the elderly couple. She hugged him and he embraced her, and they wished each other a Merry Christmas.

The woman behind me sniffled. I turned toward her and this time we both smiled.

As the couple walked toward the door, "talking" to each other, their fingers waving excitedly, the crowd shouted well wishes and a spontaneous round of applause broke out, directed at the woman who had returned to her position behind the counter.

"My daughter's deaf," she said.

I moved up another step.

5. Just a Little Bit of Cancer

Janet Morris Grimes

I SCHEDULED MY SURGERY TO REMOVE A SMALL TUMOR ON Wednesday, December 19, 2001. It would be quick and easy. Besides, it was the only time I could squeeze it into our family's busy Christmas schedules. Crystal and Andrew, our fifteen- and thirteen-year-old kids, had just completed a maddening week of exams and were thankful for the respite of Christmas break. Most of the Christmas activities and parties were behind us, including the school party for my second grader, Malloree. And if there was a quiet week at work for me that would be the one.

I chose the surgery on an outpatient basis, downplaying the entire incident by joking with the kids about how much I was looking forward to the long nap that anesthesia would provide. I envisioned a day or two for recovery and rest before I rushed to the mall to catch up on shopping, gift-wrapping, and completing Christmas preparations.

Two months earlier, I had gone to the doctor because of terrible pain in my feet, made worse by the fact that I spent hours on them with my job as an event coordinator for a local university. Dr. Clapp checked my feet and they were fine, but during his exam he noticed a lump on my neck that a previous doctor had advised was nothing to worry about.

"With close proximity to the lymph nodes," Dr. Clapp said,

"I urge you to get a CT scan and bring me the results." The result of the scan was "Requires additional investigation," which led me to a specialist who called the lump in the salivary glands in my neck a small tumor. "I recommend surgery as soon as possible," he said.

Despite his wanting me to have it done immediately, I considered it an inconvenience that I could have done in a few hours.

On the morning of December 19, my husband, Thomas, and I went to the hospital and he waited with me until a nurse wheeled me on a gurney through a series of doors and long corridors. I drifted off to sleep.

The long nap I had anticipated was interrupted by the beeping noises of hospital machinery and a few welcomed voices. Fighting the brightness of the overhead lights, I strained to open my eyes. Without my glasses, I barely discerned the faces of Thomas, our daughter Crystal, and my sister, Jeanna. Surprised at their presence, I attempted to smile but drifted out again. This cycle repeated itself as I detected broken pieces of conversation.

Nurses came and left my room. Each time I asked a question, I dozed again before it was answered. Later in the day I learned that I would have to stay overnight in the hospital. I mentally played out all the possibilities about where the kids would stay for the night but then did nothing about it.

When I was finally awake long enough to hold a conversation with the doctor, he explained that just as they were completing the surgery, test results came back showing that the tumor was malignant.

The results surprised him, but he chose not to remove the lymph nodes because that would severely disfigure my neck and shoulder area on the left side. As it was, the nerves were completely severed, so I was left with a slight facial paralysis. Too groggy to process that information, I maneuvered around the drainage tubes coming from my neck, as well as the IV still in my arm, to get comfortable. I felt sorry for everyone who was dealing with the news without me. My heart broke when I heard Jeanna and Crystal crying together in the hallway.

Thomas made calls on his cell phone to deliver the news to relatives across the country. He often teared up and his voice quivered each time he said the word *cancer*.

I wandered in and out of sleep. By the time I came out of the fog, I was home and news had spread. Our family was bombarded with visits from meal-bearing friends.

Although I still had a disgusting drainage tube coming from my neck, the kids overlooked it as we enjoyed the time at home by simply being together. We put together jigsaw puzzles, played cards, or piled up on the couch to watch our favorite Christmas specials.

Everyone seemed more concerned than I was. A couple of days after returning home, as I was doing a load of laundry, the tears suddenly began to fall. I stood with my head in my hands, the washing machine twisting through its cycle even though I hadn't put the clothes inside, and its sound drowned out my sobs.

I had cancer.

But that was it. By the end of my laundry room meltdown, I came to terms with my diagnosis, taking the same approach as I had prior to the surgery: I did not have time for cancer to take over my life. My little bit of cancer had been removed, so technically, it was gone. To our knowledge, it had not spread, so that was even more reason to celebrate and move on.

Christmas of 2001 will long be referred to as one of our best, although I don't recall what happened to my vital to-do list during that week. Thomas ordered the Christmas cards, and by the time I addressed and mailed them they probably arrived a day or two late. Nothing stands out about any gifts the children received that year, or even what Thomas and I exchanged.

I learned that on the night before my surgery the worship service at church became an hour-long prayer session just for me. That I remember.

On Christmas Eve, I walked into church with my bandaged neck, my Santa hat and matching red sweater, and my beautiful family beside me. We sang songs about the miracle of Jesus' birth, and we lit candles that reflected in our glistening eyes. We held hands and prayed together. And we hugged everyone around us. We celebrated with those who had participated in the journey.

I smiled my crooked-but-improving smile all the way home, marveling at how a little bit of cancer may have been the greatest Christmas gift of all. That extra dose of perspective reminded a too-busy family of what is most important in life.

Until then I had been consumed with doing, doing, doing. "I don't have time for this," had been a strong statement of my life, as if I could make every decision about what went on in my life. I'm still the same person, but I've learned that life is more than doing and rushing to the next project.

This life is for enjoying and for loving. It wasn't a lesson I wanted to learn, but it was certainly one I needed to grasp.

6. The Change Purse

Lisa-Anne Wooldridge

THE CLASSROOM DOOR WAS AJAR—SOMETHING I HADN'T noticed before. As I filed by for recess with my classmates, I peeked inside. I'd heard stories about the children in that room, and occasionally I'd even seen them when we stood in the lunch line.

They were a disturbing sight to our fourth- and fifth-grade classes, painful to watch as they struggled down the hallway, some in wheelchairs, others walking with bent limbs and unsteady gaits. The teachers on whom they leaned never made eye contact with us and pretended they didn't hear the whispers or nervous, muffled laughter.

Today they and the children seemed hidden away in their cozy classroom. As recess started I stood outside and peered though the glass doors. I felt strangely connected to the children inside. We weren't being monitored by our teacher, so I knocked lightly on the door.

Mrs. Lacey opened the door and stared at me. "Do you have a message from the office?" she asked.

Embarrassed, I shook my head.

"Would you like to come in?" she asked kindly.

"Yes, ma'am."

It was a small-town school. The entire special education department was housed in one room, with all ages and ranges of disabilities taught together. Some of the children smiled; some were unable to respond or seemed unaware of my presence.

One student, named John, caught my attention. He was as large as a grown man but looked entirely helpless. He was slumped over in his wheelchair with what I later learned was severe cerebral palsy. Mrs. Lacey patted his shoulder and told me that he was only four years old in his mind.

With small, jerking movements he raised his head and tried to say hello. His twin sister, Anne, who also had cerebral palsy, waved shyly.

I can't explain what happened, only that I felt a ripping pain in my heart as tears threatened to run down my face.

Mrs. Lacey smiled at me. "Would you like to help?"

I nodded enthusiastically.

After that, each day she left the door ajar and I'd walk inside while my class went to recess. And each day I'd get in line with my group when they went back to class. (In retrospect, I think my teacher probably knew about my detour, but she never said a word.)

I enjoyed doing small jobs for Mrs. Lacey, tracing coloring pages with a thick, dark line so the students with poor vision could see the images. Sometimes I demonstrated shoe tying by guiding fingers until they mastered the difficult task. I played games with the children, talked to them, gave many hugs, and made up a fun game for brushing teeth.

I really loved the special ed class. We celebrated each small victory and cheered every simple gain. Before long, I believed that the profoundly disabled could do so much more than anyone suspected. No matter how severely limited their communication abilities, each one thrived when shown love and given the chance to love back.

Those daily fifteen minutes were a happy time for me—the highlight of my school day. Being with that special class of students became more important to me than my own lessons.

By the time Christmas vacation came around, I felt as if I belonged with them. They were learning to sing beautiful carols for the holiday program, and their parents bought them red sweaters. Mrs. Lacey invited me to their class party.

Each year our school hosted a Santa's Workshop that provided the opportunity for students to buy gifts. Everything was priced out of my reach. Every day cheerful "elves" arrived to deliver presents, but I felt a deep sense of regret and sadness. I was worried that my friends in the special ed class would be left out or neglected. I hoped they didn't know about Santa's Workshop and that children in other classrooms received presents.

I was working on math when the elves came to our classroom. I was surprised to see Mrs. Lacey come in with them and she handed me a nicely wrapped package. I thanked her but felt even worse about not being able to give the gifts I'd mentally picked out for her class. I was close to tears as she gave me a smile and embraced me.

I waited until recess that day, the package hidden inside my coat pocket. The door was slightly open, reminding me of my standing invitation.

It was the day of their class party, but I didn't expect the excited greeting I received. "They want you to celebrate with them," Mrs. Lacey said.

I pulled the unopened package out of my pocket and looked at them, all beaming, especially John, who could barely hold his head up.

As if she could read my mind, Mrs. Lacey told me how thoughtful it was for me to open my present there, so they could see how much I liked it. She told me the class had gone on a field trip to Santa's Workshop and voted to buy me a present. As I unwrapped it, she told me the rest.

John had insisted they buy me a small, beautifully beaded change purse. He had no way to know it was the one gift I'd admired and wanted. That afternoon they went home and either took money from their piggy banks or asked their parents for money. Mrs. Lacey helped them as they proudly counted out their change to buy my change purse. They also selected and paid for the paper and ribbon to wrap it.

"This is the first time they've ever sent a present to anyone in the school, or felt they were part of the Christmas fun," she said.

I hugged each one of them and said each time how much I treasured the purse.

Mrs. Lacey followed me into the hall. She was so wise and seemed to understand when I didn't have the words I needed. "You are a friend of God, and you gave the children and me a gift—even if you didn't know it."

I began to cry and she cried as well. For perhaps a full minute, we stood hugging and crying in the hallway.

Before I moved away she said, "It's rare for other children to see the treasures in my classroom and to believe my students could do anything with enough love and patience and help from a friend."

I cried again.

She held my change purse up. "It doesn't matter if you never have any money to put in it. This purse is filled up with love, and as long as you give that away it will never be empty."

As beautiful as that time was in my life, it faded from memory as I grew up, moved away, married, and had my own children.

The memory came back one day as I went to feed the parking meter at a special clinic. My son had just been diagnosed with several disabilities, probably the result of being born prematurely.

I opened my change purse to get coins for the meter. That's when I remembered that other change purse—my Christmas present from long ago. Tears ran down my cheeks—happy, peaceful tears.

God spoke to my heart as if He actually said, "When you were still a child, I prepared you for this day and what your son will go through."

With sudden clarity, I realized I could focus on the treasure in my son instead of what was wrong with him. I could believe that with love, patience, and the help of a friend he could overcome anything.

My heart, like my purse, was full of love just like it was that special Christmas.

7. No More Crooked Star

Janet Perez Eckles

ANOTHER SLEEPLESS NIGHT, AND I DABBED MY TEARS WITH the corner of my pillowcase. "I hate my life," I protested to God. "I want this torment to end."

But there was no end, no relief, and no change. With no warning, an incurable retinal disease had robbed me of my eyesight. It left me without hope of medication, treatment, or cure.

"No warning for my blindness and no answer from God," I cried out. At age thirty-one, I had only anguish, pain, and three little boys who still needed me. And my loving husband, who didn't know how to help me.

My sons romped in the family room. "Mommy, I wanna drink." My three-year-old tugged at me.

I had learned to recognize each of their voices, but my new life in darkness was foreign and I struggled to do the simplest things.

Each day my frustration turned to anger. I groped for items throughout the house. I winced in pain after I smashed into open cabinet doors or fell against the furniture.

"I hate my life," I cried. "It's so unfair. Why did this happen to me?"

I didn't get any better. After three months of despair, a friend invited me to her church. Seated in the pew, I dared to hope for a miracle or any encouragement to ease my heartache.

Instead, I heard Bible verses, testimonies, and singing. I wondered if they would be singing and talking about God's love if they were blind like me.

I hardly listened to the sermon until a verse the pastor quoted seemed to leap out just for me: "Seek the Kingdom of God above all else, and live righteously, and He will give you everything you need" (Matthew 6:33).

I can't explain what happened and I don't feel I need to try, but for the first time since my blindness, my physical problem wasn't my central thought. For the first time I realized what I had to do. I had to make God my priority and "he will give you everything you need."

I decided to do exactly what Jesus commanded. I had known God when I was healthy, and now I needed to find Him again when I wasn't. I prayed, attended church, and listened to the Bible on tape.

Courage, determination, and added faith replaced my bitterness, anger, and self-centeredness. My sons saw me smile again. I slowly learned to navigate through the kitchen. I fumbled my way to prepare simple meals, such as peanut butter and jelly sandwiches, spaghetti, or other pasta. I did the laundry, cleaned their rooms, and disciplined them when needed. They also adjusted to a mommy who couldn't see.

Although daily routines became easier, Christmas season brought new experiences of frustration. The days were gone when I drove to the mall and came home with armfuls of gifts for everyone, decorated the house, wrapped packages with matching bows on each box, and arranged each ornament on the fresh pine tree. I could no longer do any of that—I had to relinquish those tasks to my husband. And he never complained.

In the silence of one night just before Christmas, while the family slept, I sat on the couch in front of the Christmas tree. As always, a veil of dark gray blocked any glimpse of the lights, the ornaments, and the reds and greens that make Christmas come alive. I bit my lip in irritation because I had no way to see if the star atop the tree was straight.

This gloom will rule the rest of my Christmases, I said to myself. I inhaled a long breath and my stomach cramped with grief.

"Stop it," I said aloud. "You know better and you don't have to feel sorry for yourself. You're alive." I tried to reason and to become optimistic as I fought self-pity. But the desire to see again, especially at this special time of year, refused to be pushed away.

I headed to bed asking God for strength, a bit of comfort, and peace. I still had no peace.

Christmas morning came, and three pairs of little feet bounced around our bed.

"I want to open presents!" our oldest called out.

"Me, too!" his brothers added.

I ran my hand to the end of the bed to find my robe, slipped it on, and followed their voices. As I entered our family room, the pine scent filled the air and the joy of my little boys filled my heart.

"Okay, we have to do this in order," I instructed. "Daddy will give one present to each of you and you'll open it when we tell you to do so."

My youngest slipped off the couch. "Me first." He tore off the wrapping, placing paper and scraps on my lap. "This is cool!" he screamed. I turned in his direction. Everything in me longed to see the expression on his little face.

What did he open? What made him so excited?

I swallowed the lump in my throat and chided myself—why couldn't I just enjoy what I heard? But the more they oohed and aahed, the more my longing to see overwhelmed me.

"I'll be right back." I rose from the couch and with arms stretched out, following the wall, I headed to my bedroom.

I sat on my bed and tears flowed.

Lord, why is this affecting me so? Please help me to understand. Show me how to cope. I don't know how.

While I tried to muffle my sobs, my husband came in and put his arms around me. "What can I do for you, honey?"

"I'm okay." I brushed my cheek with the back of my hand. I was lying, but I didn't want him to suffer.

"Mommy, Daddy, can we open some more?" the boys called out.

I turned to my husband. "You go ahead. I'll be there in a minute. I don't want to ruin things."

I yanked a tissue from the box on our dresser.

"This is the best present of all!" one of them squealed.

His voice carried such conviction, passion, and sincerity. Without realizing it, his words carried a sobering message for me. He had found his favorite present.

By dwelling on what I couldn't see, I had missed *my* special present. I had overlooked the Christmas gift God placed before me—Jesus, the Savior.

8. Christmas Rainbow

Susan Miura

THE AROMAS OF GARLIC AND OLIVE OIL, STEAMED CRAB, and buttery shrimp mingled together in my family's kitchen as we prepared for the evening. On the table, bottles of lemon juice and Tabasco sauce stood like sentries next to a pile of gray clams nestled on a bed of crushed ice. In a traditional Sicilian family, Christmas Eve means a feast of seven kinds of fish, a huge pot of *aglio e oglio* (garlic pasta), and a noisy, multigenerational gathering that ends with midnight mass.

After each ring of the doorbell, I was showered by hugs and kisses as relatives came with gifts and food. Lively discussions about the past year filled the house. That year, 1964, had been packed with events, although being only six years old, I didn't care about most of them.

"What do you think of Elizabeth Taylor marrying Richard Burton?" Mom chatted with my aunt as she arranged stuffed artichokes on a platter.

"How about them Beatles?" My uncle slapped his forehead in disgust. "*Madonna*, that long hair is crazy!"

Dad heartily nodded his agreement as he drained the spaghetti.

"I saw *Mary Poppins*!" I thought it was the best movie ever, but I'm not sure anyone heard me.

News turned to nostalgia when my mother brought up what Christmas used to be like in the "old neighborhood"—an Italian section next to Chicago's Chinatown.

"All of us cousins piled into the back of a pickup truck and belted out carols while someone drove us to mass," she said. "There was no fear of getting pulled over for making so much noise because there were fewer laws back then." She smiled and added, "We Italians had plenty of our own laws. Messing with them would have dire consequences."

I knew from hearing a thousand stories that one of those "laws" concerned marriage. My parents, like their relatives and friends, assumed their children would marry Italians. As strong as that sounds, my parents were less stringent than the previous generation, who insisted on marrying someone from the same *region* of Italy. Those who didn't abide by that rule were often alienated from their own families.

As Dad said, "Red-hot Sicilian blood flowed through every man, woman, and nana at those Christmas Eve gatherings."

And it stayed that way until Christmas Eve 1966.

Something seemed different about my sister that Christmas Eve. Patt was anxious for dinner to begin and rounded up the slow-moving relatives and hurried them to the table.

Immediately after the prayer, she clinked her fork against a glass to get everyone's attention. "Roger and I are engaged!"

His name was Roger Chase.

"But he's not Italian," Dad said after everyone had left. "And he's not even Catholic."

"He eats pizza with a knife and fork and stares at artichokes like they came from a distant planet," Mom said.

Roger was English and Finnish, and he was Lutheran.

"I will not attend the nuptials," Nana, my grandmother, said. (At my father's insistence she eventually relented.)

I would be a flower girl and I was more excited about that than the arguing around the table.

That was the first nontraditional wedding in our family.

It wasn't the last.

In 1973, I wore a slick copper-colored gown as my brother Chuck married his college sweetheart, Dori. She didn't have a drop of Sicilian blood in her, either, but Dad made sure Nana came to that wedding, too—even though a rabbi conducted the ceremony.

Eventually I realized that Dad was a renegade who broke the barriers of the prejudiced world in which he grew up. A few years later, my other brother, Joe, stood in a sunny courtyard and married Sharon, a Wisconsin girl of German descent. He lovingly and happily adopted her four-year-old daughter.

After that, Christmas Eves at our house were filled with the laughter and tears of beautiful half-Italian babies. Mom and Dad opened their hearts and arms to our family's new additions but still clung to the hope that I, their baby, would finally bring home a *paisan.*

I didn't. Instead, I got lost in the deep-brown eyes of a Japanese police officer named Gary and married him.

With thoughts of their own monocultural upbringing, my parents were concerned my children might be ostracized for their mixed race. I never felt it and neither did Gary. Our son had scores of friends from a rainbow of nationalities.

On Christmas Eve 1996, we gathered as always before a table laden with traditional seafood and pasta. As my sister did years before, I waited not so patiently for everyone to be seated and say grace. After thanking God for the miracle of His Son and the love we shared as a family, I made my announcement: "A second Japanese-Italian is coming this way."

Cheers and clapping filled the room, but my mother stayed silent; tears shimmered in her eyes as she smiled and squeezed my hand. The phrase "mixed race" no longer applied. She was getting another precious grandchild, and that's what mattered.

With each Christmas gathering, our melting pot simmered with rich new flavors and colors of those who had joined our family during the year. And as the grandchildren grew and married, a new generation of young people entered the mix, none of them from any corner of Italy. In fact, some of them were adopted or from other countries.

In May 2009, the one who started it all by proposing to my mother sixty-five years earlier lost his life to lung cancer.

Grief knows no cultural boundaries. In that little church on a Thursday afternoon, people from all walks of life came to honor a man who had impacted innumerable lives without thought of ethnicity or color. In the months that followed, God again demonstrated His unfailing goodness by blessing our family with three healthy babies—sweet little faces that helped us find joy and strength in the midst of our grief.

Seven months later we gathered for our first Christmas Eve without our beloved patriarch. We had the traditional bowls of shrimp and *aglio e oglio*, but they were joined by Costa Rican salad, Mexican *pico de gallo*, Peruvian *aji*, and other delicious representations of our multicultural family.

There was great joy, as always, during these gatherings, but there was an unmistakable void. Dad wasn't there to greet each person with a bear hug, dish out pasta, or tell corny jokes. And yet his spirit was strong in that room as we celebrated the birth of Jesus Christ, who told his followers, "Love each other. Just as I have loved you, you should love each other" (Jn. 13:34). There were no caveats regarding skin color or country of origin. His command was simple: "Love each other."

And so we do.

9. A Timely Surprise

Linda Gilden

WHERE COULD IT BE? I KNOW I PUT THAT TABLECLOTH IN this closet, right on this shelf in front of me. How could I have lost it?

It wasn't really a tablecloth; it was a tablecloth kit.

As I was growing up, one of my favorite Christmas traditions was carefully placing Mama's cross-stitched tablecloth on our dining room table. A year's worth of fold lines ran through holly leaves and bright red poinsettias. After running to the kitchen to wash our hands, we finger-pressed each crease and smoothed every tiny wrinkle.

Mama knew how much my sister and I loved that tablecloth. So on a summer trip, she and Daddy found a sewing shop where they bought us cross-stitch tablecloth kits. The finished product would look similar to her own tablecloth.

My sister and I were so excited. Not being an enthusiastic seamstress, I put mine in the closet until I was mentally ready to undertake such a task. I liked to cross-stitch, but I had done little of it since the births of my children. But after all, it was then only summer and I would have plenty of time before Christmas.

The time came when I realized that if I was going to complete the tablecloth by the holidays I had to start soon. I set aside time to make my own Christmas tablecloth.

But I couldn't find the kit.

I looked at the shelves in my closet, a chronicle of many years as a pack rat. The wooden "little people" that for years were individually named as my children played with them lay inside a blue plastic bucket. I had stacked framed pictures dating back to my mother's first dance recital, separated and protected by frayed beach towels. I had a large collection of record albums that once prompted my children to say, "Those are awfully big CDs."

My closet included broken telephones and appliances that challenged my son as he took them apart. My daughter's Garfield collection rested in its marked plastic box waiting its turn for display again. Three times I went through everything in the closet.

There was no tablecloth kit.

Among the family I had the reputation as being the family I-can't-keep-up-with-anything member. Would I have to confess the tablecloth had joined the ranks of the unaccounted for at my house? How could I have been so careless with something that I wanted handed down from generation to generation?

My sister had long ago finished her tablecloth, despite being a full-time medical student. As a typical overachiever, she was adept at multitasking. For example, several times I visited her apartment and she stitched as we caught up on the news.

For a while I had been able to say I was too busy to think about sewing. But my deadline was close and I couldn't even find the tablecloth to get started. What was I going to do?

I searched again. I finally invited a friend to my house and she helped with the search. Still no tablecloth.

During the weeks before Christmas, Mama and I went shopping together, out to lunch, and decorated each other's homes.

Each time we were together I feared she would ask if I had finished my tablecloth. The closer Christmas Day came, the more nervous I was and I kept trying to figure out what to say without lying.

I never found that tablecloth kit.

In my mind I repeatedly practiced my speech about what had happened to it. I tried several excuses that shifted the blame from me to others, even the dog. But I really didn't want to tell something that wasn't true. I finally decided the best approach was just to say I hadn't had time to do it (which was true) and it was in a safe place (I didn't have to say it was so safe that even I couldn't find it). I didn't want to let on that I didn't know where it was. Besides, I knew it was somewhere in the house and surely I would find it before the next Christmas season.

Despite frequent visits to my home during the holidays, Mama never acknowledged the obvious absence of the new cross-stitched tablecloth from my dining room table. When passing through the room, she commented only on how pretty the table looked. I never had to use any of my contrived answers to respond to her question: "Where's your new tablecloth?"

On Christmas Eve, our entire family gathered as usual at Mama's house. We sat at the table for vegetable soup and the reading of the Christmas story. After that we went into the living room.

Christmas was Mama's favorite time of the year and it wasn't unusual for her ninety-eight-pound, type-A personality to move quickly from task to task. She seemed especially enthusiastic this year as we gathered beside her tree.

The one grandchild sorted the presents. That took quite a while, so we sang carols. That year as soon as we were settled on the furniture or the floor, Mama whispered to my sister. I was curious, but it didn't seem important.

After we had our designated gifts, Mama jumped up, grabbed one of the largest presents in my pile, and said, "This one! We want you to open this one first. Hurry up! Don't anyone open a gift until Linda opens this one."

That kind of thing hadn't happened before, and I thought it was delightful. Mama was so excited, I knew it would be fun.

Carefully breaking the ribbon and tearing the paper, I teased everyone by taking my time.

"Just open it," my sister said.

Still puzzled by their enthusiasm, I lifted the lid. And there it lay! My tablecloth. Each stitch perfectly crossed and each little rhinestone sewn in the middle of every poinsettia.

A few tears rolled down my cheek as I realized how much time and love had gone into making that gift. As I learned later, after my sister finished hers she had helped stitch mine. Mama had added green stems and sewed on the rhinestones. But the best part of all, of course, was they had kept the secret for months.

"My tablecloth," I said for at least the fourth time. It was my treasure, an heirloom for my children to enjoy one day.

Since then, each year my children and I carefully unfold *my* Christmas tablecloth, finger-pressing and smoothing as we go. Not only is my tablecloth beautiful; it's also a lovely reminder of a Christmas when one of my greatest frustrations yielded a precious surprise gift.

The loving spirit of Christmas moved my mother and sister to create that tablecloth for me, and I see the beauty of that spirit in each stitch and every sparkling rhinestone—beauty that many others can enjoy for generations to come.

10. A Scrooge Christmas?

Sylvia Bright-Green

I STARED AT WHAT I HELD IN MY HANDS. *THIS IS SO CRUEL,* I thought. *How could they do this to me?*

It was Christmas Eve and the others eagerly opened their wrapped gifts. Excitement and laughter filled the air.

I sat in the living room and watched my loved ones gathered around the glittering tree. As they ripped away the wrappings, I could no longer fight back my tears of hurt and rejection. The more I contemplated my Christmas gifts, while others around me laughed and enjoyed the camaraderie, the harder it was for me to control my heartbreaking tears.

I got up quietly and walked into my bedroom. I didn't turn on the lights. I wanted to be alone in my deep pain.

As I lay there and sobbed, I kept wondering why they had done such cruel things to me. Didn't I always try to make the month of December special for the family? Didn't they appreciate how deeply I loved them and how much I'd tried to give myself for their happiness? Why would our four married children give me such callous, heartless Christmas gifts?

I thought about the gifts repeatedly. No matter how I tried to explain it to myself, I couldn't find anything to laugh about. What's good about a pair of combat boots, a long, thick block of wood with sandpaper, a decorated Kleenex box filled with cans of wax, and a plastic bag of tiny ripped pieces of paper?

Do they really hate me that much? Have I failed them that badly?

At first, when I received my presents, I felt elated and involved in the merriment of the traditional holiday gift giving. However, after I opened the first package and saw the combat boots, I thought I must have received the wrong gift.

No one paid any attention to me and they seemed focused on opening their own gifts. So I opened the second, third, and fourth packages. No one said anything, but by then they had stopped and everyone stared at me.

Not knowing what else to do and feeling confused and hurt, I smiled at them. They hurried back to their own gifts.

Why? Why? Why had they given me such mean-spirited gifts?

I tried to figure out the messages they had sent me.

Were the combat boots because they thought I ran the house like a drill sergeant, always issuing orders? Was the block of wood because I acted like a blockhead when I didn't give in to their many requests or demands? The box of wax, I assumed, must be their way of telling me to "mind your own beeswax." But the fourth gift, the bag of ripped pieces of paper, meant what? Was it for stuffing something? None of the conclusions were easy to accept, but the ripped paper seemed beyond me.

Or perhaps I hurt too much to think clearly.

What did I do that was so naughty to warrant punishment from my family on Christmas Eve? Why would my beloved children be so unkind on the most precious night of the year? Where was their love for me?

Just then, a warm hand touched my back. "Honey, why are you crying?"

How could my husband of twenty-five years ask me such a ludicrous question? Didn't he know?

I turned over and stared at him. Our younger daughter, Karen, standing beside him, asked, "What's wrong?"

By then the whole family had come into our bedroom. I sat up. "You have to ask me what's wrong? Isn't it obvious? You give me a block of wood, a box of wax, a bag of ripped paper, and a pair of combat boots for Christmas, and you ask me what's wrong?"

"You forgot the sandpaper," Terri, our older daughter, said.

Everyone laughed.

I stared at their faces, trying to figure out what was going on.

Our younger son, Darin, draped his arm lovingly around my shoulder, kissed me, and said, "We love you and Dad very much, and no gift in the world could ever express or show that love."

"You mean you really don't know what those gifts are all about?" Mark, our older son, asked.

"No, I don't."

Mark took me by my arm and ushered me back to the paper-strewn living room. "I think we need to explain it to her."

"You left the room so fast," Darin said, "you never got to open the other gift that went with those items for you and Dad."

Still not clear about what was going on, I immediately regretted my outburst and said as calmly as I could, "Thank you for making me aware that Christmas is not just about presents under a decorated tree. It's about having the gift of my family around me, loving me. I'm sorry I forgot that and became so upset over my—my gifts."

"This ought to explain everything." Terri handed me a beautiful metallic gold envelope.

I opened the envelope, and on the Christmas card I read these words:

Mom, Dad, over the years you've always joked about the things you could have done if you wouldn't have married so young. Such as hiking through Yellowstone National Park, surfing in Hawaii, skiing in the Alps, or taking the Love Boat to Acapulco. That's what your gifts are all about. The boots are for hiking, the long block of wood with sandpaper is your kit representing your surfboard, the box of wax is for your skis, and the bag of ripped paper is your confetti to throw from the deck of your Love Boat. Inside this envelope is another envelope with your tickets and traveler's checks. We love you both very much for all that you have given and done for us, so Merry Christmas and Bon Voyage."

I cried again, but this time feelings of joy, of love, and of happiness flowed through me. I embraced them all. A spirit of love and appreciation filled the room.

I realized then—in a deeper way than ever—that Christmas *is* about love. And that Christmas I felt embraced by their love.

11. A Quiet Christmas Moment

Cheryl Barker

AS I WORKED IN THE KITCHEN ONE DECEMBER EVENING, AN unexpected silence filled the atmosphere. Such a quiet atmosphere settling over our normally noisy home was unusual.

My husband had gone for an evening of basketball with the guys. Shafts of light from under their doors meant our teenage daughters were in their rooms. Kristin and Kelli usually kept the house bustling with activity in the evenings, but on that night I heard nothing from their rooms.

With the holiday season making life more frenzied than usual, I needed the quiet moments when I could be alone and reflect on the purpose of this special season. Eager with anticipation, I wiped the kitchen counters clean. As I dried my hands, I listened.

The house remained still. I thought of the words of Clement Moore's well-loved Christmas poem: "Not a creature was stirring, not even a mouse."

I walked into our living room and I felt as if a comforting sight welcomed me with a warm embrace. The beauty of the room was illuminated only by the lights on our Christmas tree. The glow spread to a corner of the piano where I had placed a small country church. As I surveyed the room, everything around me whispered, "Peace."

I feel I've stumbled into a silent, holy night.

Contentment washed over me, filling my soul. For several seconds, I closed my eyes as if I could permanently soak in everything. *Christmas . . . my home . . . my family . . . my memories . . . my Savior.*

After I gazed at the tree, thoughts of things I could be doing interrupted my solitude. I had other chores—and those never ended. As it was Christmas season, I had gifts to wrap, Christmas cards to write, and our favorite holiday foods to cook.

My mind became the enemy of my silent, holy night. Would I allow my peace to be snatched from me by the distractions of unfinished tasks? Or could I accept that quiet moment as a gift and take time to celebrate Christmas in the sanctuary of our living room?

Sinking down into my favorite spot on the sofa, I stared at the tree. My gaze wandered from ornament to ornament. Each one held a special memory. Some had been in my husband's family for years; others were mementos of family vacations. A few had come as gifts from family and friends. After only a few minutes, the feelings of nostalgia turned to a spirit of worship as I focused on the ornaments that reminded me of the birth of Jesus.

As my gaze shifted from the tree to my little lighted church and back to the tree again, a sense of wonder overwhelmed me. I considered the magnitude of what God did for us on that long-ago night in Bethlehem. He changed the world with the gift of His Son. That humble beginning brought hope to all generations and eternal life for all who believe.

Joy and love for my Savior welled up inside me, and I softly sang a few carols of Christmas—the songs that so beautifully expressed my praise and adoration.

While singing "Silent Night," I stared at our manger scene. Part of that area remained in the dark, and I couldn't see it clearly. I smiled as I thought, *I really want to see Bethlehem right now.* As if in answer to my desire, the atmosphere of wonder and worship surrounding me increased, engulfing my homemade sanctuary with God's presence.

As I continued singing, my eyes adjusted to the darkness and the manger scene came into focus. In my mind's eye, I saw Mary and Joseph kneeling in worship near the baby Jesus. With amazing clarity, I watched as an angel hovered overhead; an ambassador of heaven kept watch. Silent animals seemed to sense the sacredness of that peaceful scene. This was the miracle of Christmas. And I felt I was experiencing it for the first time.

A few minutes earlier, when my first notes of the carols broke the silence around me, I wondered what my teenagers would think if they walked in and caught their mother singing in the glow of the Christmas tree. I smiled and decided I didn't care. God had given me a special gift in the quiet moments of Christmas.

After several minutes passed and my heart filled with the quiet peace and deep joy of true Christmas celebration, I thanked God for giving me an unexpected opportunity to worship. I hoped that others, too, would listen to their hearts and take time in the middle of the holiday rush to reflect on the miracle of Christmas and experience that Holy Night once again.

Something powerful happened to me in the midst of those quiet moments. I perceived Christmas in a deeper, more profound way than I had since I was a child. I decided to make space each Christmas season for a quiet, reflective time.

In the years ahead I'll sit near my tree, gaze at the nativity scene once more, and ask God to join me in another silent, holy night.

12. Gracie and the Eight-foot Pine Tree

Shirley Reynolds

ON OUR KNEES AMONG DIRT AND ROCKS, MY HUSBAND, KEN, and I planned to transform our front yard into something beautiful. We gathered rakes, clippers, and yard bags and began the task. I stood at the end of our property and surveyed the situation.

"Maybe we should have hired someone to do this job?" I said.

"Nah," he said. "Come on. It'll be the best on the block."

I knelt down and began digging holes in the dry soil for the multitude of flowers. Hours later, after I had planted the last of the shrubs in the ground, a loud voice interrupted my tranquil thoughts.

Gracie, our neighbor, yelled out her window, "What's the commotion out there? Not planting trees between our houses are you?"

Smiling, I waved. "We're putting in tam junipers. They will look great; don't worry." Then I added, "Hey, would you like to go to church with us Sunday morning?"

Gracie frowned and slammed her window shut.

"Guess not," I said.

A few feet away, a six-inch pine tree lay with its root endings exposed. I picked up the sad specimen. "Our first tree." I held it up, dug a hole, packed it with topsoil, and placed the bedraggled tree in the hole. "There, great, don't you think?" I said to my husband. "We'll call it the branch."

I had to giggle, thinking the branch didn't have a chance of surviving, but it was fun.

After a full day of planting, weeding, and clearing brush, we sat on our backyard deck with glasses of lemonade. Stretching our legs out on our lounge chairs, we laughed about the branch.

"That thing isn't going to make it," my kind husband commented.

"I know," I said, and paused to sip my drink. "But God does work miracles."

To our surprise, the branch survived. As the years passed, the branch defied nature and grew heartily in the hard, rocky soil. Since we lived in Seattle, it received an enormous amount of rain. It never had the benefit of fertilizers or plant food, but much to our surprise, it grew.

One morning, while looking out the front room window, I noticed that the top of our once-spindly pine tree had grown to the height of a small Christmas tree.

"Hey, Ken, that tree is bigger than I thought it would grow. And it's perfectly shaped. Like God is growing it for Christmas."

A few weeks later, I received a phone call from Gracie. "Better pull that tree out by the roots!" she yelled. "It will drop branches on my roof one day!"

"It'll never grow that big." Even as I said those words, I wasn't so sure.

Gracie grumbled some more, and before she hung up she said, "I told you not to plant a tree between the houses."

By the next fall, I stared at the pine tree and saw that it had reached past the window. Ken and I walked outside and took a long look. It was now an eight-foot evergreen.

"It would make a gorgeous Christmas tree for the church," I said.

Ken shook his head, saying, "There's too much sentimental value wrapped up in that tree to cut it down."

Later that same day, Gracie came to our house. "When are you getting that eyesore out of your yard? It will take over. When the winter snow comes that thing will drop branches and needles all over the top of my roof."

I didn't know what to say and I didn't think she would listen anyway.

"I'll cut it down if you don't!" She turned around and walked back to her house.

One evening, Ken answered the door and again it was Gracie. "Good evening," he said kindly. "Coming to church on Sunday?"

"It's not a good evening and no, I am not going to church on Sunday. There are branches from that tree of yours on my roof. I called the city maintenance crew to cut it down tomorrow. I thought I'd let you know."

As soon as Gracie was gone, I asked Ken, "She can't do that, can she?"

"I'm afraid she can if there's a problem with it being in the way."

Sad though I was, I began to pray for Gracie. She seemed so unhappy. Even though she had refused our invitations, I decided to invite her to our Christmas service, because I was sure she would enjoy the Christmas music.

Saturday morning the sound of a chain saw awakened us. I grabbed my robe, ran outside, and saw a maintenance crew ready to go to work.

"This is our property," I said. "You can't just come here and cut this tree down."

Gracie yelled across the yard, "Oh yes, they can. It's the law. Your tree's been declared an obstruction!"

I walked into the house in tears. "I'm crying over the branch. It's just . . . it's just special." I thought of the miracle of its survival and how Ken and I had watched it grow almost inch by inch.

After the crew downed the tree, my husband placed it in the back of the crew's flatbed truck and told me he'd be gone for a while.

As I watched out the window, he walked to Gracie's front door. With the windows open, I heard their voices.

"We've been praying for you, Gracie. Won't you come to the Christmas program at church?" Before she had a chance to respond, my sweet husband leaned over and hugged her.

Stunned, she began to cry. "I . . . I want to come. It's just that . . . I lost both my husband and daughter two Christmases ago and your blooming evergreen tree constantly reminded me of our last Christmas tree." She backed inside and closed her door.

I stood by the window during the entire time. I wanted to be angry, but I couldn't. Instead, my tears flowed. I realized that my Christmas spirit had flown away somewhere between the thud of the tree and my grumpy neighbor.

"Forgive me, God," I prayed.

Peace slowly filled my heart.

✳ ✳ ✳

Christmas was two weeks away, and our church prepared for its yearly celebration. The congregation held a dress rehearsal and afterward would gather to decorate the Christmas tree that would stand at the front of the church.

I still prayed for Gracie and asked God to forgive my attitude. "And please, Lord, bring her to church."

On Sunday morning, as Ken and I stepped inside the church sanctuary, I commented on the Christmas tree, "Isn't the tree the most beautiful one they've ever decorated?"

Ken stood absolutely quiet beside me. "It is a gem, isn't it?" he said. "You know what, it looks a lot like our branch on the top, don't you think?"

I looked more carefully. A smile formed on my face and tears filled my eyes. I squeezed his hand, glad that he had donated the branch to our church.

"I think God is doing some big miracles in my heart," I said. "There was a reason for cutting it down, wasn't there?"

"Yes, there was." A few minutes later, Ken turned around to look at the rear of the building. "And look in the back of the church—"

Gracie smiled and walked toward us.

"Merry Christmas, Gracie!" I got up and held out my arms to embrace her.

"I'm so sorry," she said.

"It's okay. You're here, and God is still working miracles!"

I embraced her. She turned her face away, but I saw the glistening tears on her face. And I thought that, much like the branch growing out of that hostile soil, Gracie was growing past her hard, stony attitude toward her neighbors.

It had taken her a while to get the Christmas spirit, but as she sat next to me, the magic of the season filled my own heart as well. I silently thanked God that I had been chosen to help open her heart.

13. From One Angel to Another

Del Bates

"I KNOW WE OFFERED TO CHAIR THE ANGEL TREE PROGRAM this year," Janice said from the other end of the phone, "but there's so much going on, and I can't do it."

The Angel Tree had been part of our Christmas season for as long as Jon and I had been married. Before we met, he was the coordinator at the church. Once we were married, I had volunteered to work with him. Although we were no longer members of that congregation, Jon volunteered again because they couldn't find enough volunteers to keep the project afloat.

For the next few years we coordinated it on our own by calling on local pastors who we believed had a heart for that kind of ministry. The most important thing was to be sure that *every* child received a gift.

I stress that because we know the gifts they received from the church might be the *only* gifts those special children would have for Christmas. Their mothers or fathers were incarcerated. Through Prison Fellowship, the ministry called Angel Tree reached out through local churches to see that these innocent children had a Christmas. The program spread across the country and often includes any poor families, but we had a special group for our Angel Tree outreach.

After two years of Jon and me juggling it on our own, my dear friend Janice called one day. "My husband and I would like to take over Angel Tree this year," she said. "We've talked to our pastor and he's willing to promote it through our church. What do you think?"

I was delighted and said, "Let's get together so Jon and I can hand over everything to you and Steve."

Things went well. The gifts came in and they were delivered. Many happy children received presents in the name of their parent and Jesus Christ. Then, the next year came. Same idea. Same plan until I received that desperate phone call from Janice. I didn't know how to respond since *my* calendar was already full. I had berated myself for taking so many responsibilities at Christmas. How was I supposed to find time so late to tie the strings on this one?

Janice shared her problems—and they were immense. As I listened to her heartaches, mine began to fade. I couldn't turn her down.

"Just tell me where you are, and Jon and I will take over. Don't worry. Everything will be fine." I hoped I knew what I was saying.

From then on, everything shifted into fifth gear. I still recall Steve backing into our driveway with his black SUV loaded with all kinds of toys, from dolls to tricycles and trains. After everything was unpacked and carried inside, I might have thought I'd just stepped into a child's magical toy land.

Jon and I needed to get to work. The first task was to wrap each gift and gather the right toys together by family name. I thanked God for the long hallway inside our house. Time was running out, but God was on our side. Eventually every gift was counted, re-counted, and ready to go. After several years of practice, Jon knew the streets of our city. He'd organize the deliveries in such a way that every present would be out within a day or two.

We finally delivered presents from one side of town to the other, except for one. We couldn't find the house for one particular family, so I called the number on the application.

"Hello, this is Juanita," a soft-spoken voice answered. "How can I help you?"

"We have Christmas presents for your children and we need directions."

She told us how to get there. Within minutes we arrived at a run-down house with kids peeking out the windows or hiding in the yard.

Juanita stood at the door and welcomed us into her home. The response was probably the warmest we had received that day. The gratitude that poured forth from her and her children warmed our hearts like the kindling flame of a winter's fire.

The kids excitedly helped us carry the presents inside. As we were leaving, Juanita commented, "I noticed gifts for my sons, but I didn't see anything for my two older daughters. I hate to ask," she added, "but did you forget them?"

I didn't have the heart to say that Angel Tree only provided gifts to the younger ones and stopped when they reached sixteen. Instead I asked, "What are their names, and what do you think they'd want?"

Juanita suggested a few ideas and Jon and I were on our way. Once we got inside the car, we looked at each other and said, "Off to the mall again." But something was different this time. We weren't shopping for a name on an application. We were shopping for faces. We shopped for a family that didn't have a tree, a dinner, and who knew as I did that Christmas was only a few days away.

At that moment, God began to work on my heart. *We have an extra tree with all the decorations packed away that I don't even use anymore. I'll bet those girls would love to decorate some of the cutout cookies I just baked.* My mind started to whirl from groceries to cleaning out my closet and even to old games that were packed away and no longer played.

Two days later Jon and I returned with our gifts. Juanita's eyes twinkled as she saw the purple and silver ornaments neatly tucked into the huge plastic bin. "Purple is my favorite color," she said. "How did you know?"

I didn't, but God did. And God also knew that she had no groceries stored up for Christmas dinner. Before Jon and I left, we asked Juanita what time would be good for us to stop by the next day and deliver Christmas dinner for the family.

I thought she was going to cry, but she didn't. She blinked several times and finally said, "Um . . . noon . . . one . . . two— whatever works best for you."

Noon it was. The next day, the aroma of turkey and dressing continued to lift our spirits as we pulled into the drive. But what was different? The screened-in porch that once seemed dark and dreary glowed from within.

"Are those our lights?" I asked Jon. "Those kids sure work fast!"

While we waited for Juanita to open the door, the sounds of joyous children came from inside. Just as we started to question what was going on, the door inched open. The kids had scrambled around to get the tree lit before they let us come inside.

Once we were inside, my gaze was drawn to our old familiar tree that glistened from the corner of their living room. Although each bulb wasn't strategically placed as I used to do it, I thought, *Who cares?*

As we handed the boxes of food to Juanita, tears filled her eyes. Seconds later she reached for a present from under the tree and placed it in our hands. "This is for you. We could never thank you for all that you've done, but God can."

Although we tried to refuse, she was determined that we should take it, so we did.

As we drove away, I opened it up. "I don't believe it!" I exclaimed. "The very thing we made sure we included in their presents . . ."

"What is it?" Jon asked.

With tears streaming down my face, I lifted out a black leather Bible from the festive Christmas paper. My mind traveled back to Juanita's words as she handed us this gift: "We could never thank you for all that you've done, but God can."

I cried as I realized what a sacrifice that must have been for her to buy me a Bible—and a leather-bound one.

I had tried to be a Christmas angel to her and her family. As tears slowly cascaded down my cheeks, I realize that Juanita had been an angel to me and showed the real spirit of Christmas. Jon and I gave out of abundance; she gave out of poverty.

14. Christmas in Cocoa Beach

Jean Matthew Hall

IN 1977, JERRY AND I WERE ON THE STAFF OF A SMALL, STRUG-gling Christian school in Cocoa Beach, Florida. Our salaries were a pittance, and several times the school's funds were so low we didn't get a check on payday. That meant scrimping with the only expenditure over which we had any real control—the grocery bill. We ate a lot of oatmeal that year.

Each evening we read the Bible with our sons and prayed together for God to provide the things we needed. We were teaching them that they could trust God to keep His promises.

As Christmas drew near, we faced the reality that we had absolutely no money. With our December paychecks we gave a tenth of our income—which was our custom—made our mobile-home payment and took care of our lot rent, paid our utilities, and put gasoline in our car. That left us nothing for groceries and nothing for Christmas.

Each night I pulled something together from whatever was in our pantry, usually oatmeal or biscuits, hot dogs, or cheap frozen pizzas.

Ten days before Christmas the cupboard and the refrigerator were both almost empty.

We continued faithfully to ask God to supply what we needed. But, after the lights were out for the night and I had tucked the blankets around Stephen and David, who were sleeping soundly, and after Jerry had fallen asleep, I fell apart: *Where are you, God? We've given ourselves to You and You promised to provide. This isn't much of a provision.* I was worried and I cried. I could see nothing positive ahead for us. I pleaded with God not to let our sons go hungry.

The last day of school before Christmas break the boys and I rushed home to relax and admire our little plastic Christmas tree. It had been given to us several years earlier by the children's home where Jerry and I had served as houseparents for three years.

Jerry had to finish his day by driving students home in the school's bus. He arrived just in time for supper. We celebrated our much-needed break with bologna sandwiches and tomato soup. The boys were excited about Christmas and the toys that were on their wish lists. Jerry and I said nothing about Christmas gifts. I didn't want to break their hearts. Jerry and I prayed together that night that God would provide a way for us to give the boys something to unwrap for Christmas.

After the boys were tucked in, Jerry went back to the school to catch up on some paperwork. Shortly after he left, someone rapped on our front door. I flipped on the outside light and peeked out the window.

I opened the door to "Uncle" George from the children's home. He held a large box. "Good evening," he said, and grinned. "Hope I'm not coming too late. We were straightening up our pantry today and realized we had too much food—it won't all fit. We wondered if you can use any of this stuff." He set the box on our table.

My eyes filled with tears as I saw cereal, pasta, crackers,

soup, canned veggies, and fresh fruit. "Yes, we sure can," I said. "Your coming is definitely an answer to prayer for us—"

"I guess you can use a little more then," George said. Just before he closed the door on his way out, he called out, "I'll be right back." He hopped down the steps and ran to his van. He brought another big box inside. Then another, and another. Each box was loaded with a variety of food. They weren't leftovers. Someone had planned carefully to be sure we got a little bit of everything we might need—including more oatmeal.

I cried my way through George's bringing in each box and tried to thank him for every item.

"I've got one more box. Have you got some room in your freezer?"

"I have any empty freezer, so there's plenty of space."

Minutes later I looked at what he had brought. *Thank you, Lord, for meat!* I thought as I placed the packages into our freezer. "Meat, orange juice, and ice cream," I said aloud. "We haven't had ice cream in a long time, George."

Apparently awakened by the noise, Stephen and David walked into the kitchen. "What's all this stuff?"

"It's God's answer to our prayers," I said.

Uncle George bent down to our sons' heights. "God always answers our prayers, boys. He knows everything we need before we even need it." One at a time, Uncle George grabbed our sons and threw them across his shoulders. They giggled as he took each one on an airplane ride in his arms.

"Thank you, Uncle George. This truly is an answer to our prayers." I was so teary eyed, I could hardly talk. "We had nothing, absolutely nothing, to eat. Your gifts mean we can really celebrate Christmas now." I wiped my tears and reached out to hug him.

"Hey, boys, I know it's bedtime, but I'll bet your mom won't mind if I give you a candy bar, will she?" He winked at me as he held a candy bar in each hand.

I nodded and smiled.

"And I'll bet she won't even care if you eat it in your rooms." The boys grabbed their candy and ran into their rooms. Two doors slammed, followed by a lot of laughter.

"I have one more thing in the van," George said quietly before he went out the front door again. Almost immediately, he returned with two gigantic plastic trash bags bulging like Santa's sack.

"The Lord blessed us with plenty of stuff for our kids for Christmas and we want to share some of it with you." He plopped the bags down and opened them. This time I couldn't hold back my tears.

I saw toy tanks, soccer balls, coloring books, cowboy hats, sweaters and socks, and a large box of candy canes. The second bag held more gifts as well as an abundance of wrapping paper.

"You might want to hide these away before they finish those candy bars and come running back in here for more. Show me where to put them." We stuffed the bags into my closet.

I followed George to his van, thanking him repeatedly.

"You know you don't have to thank us, don't you? God heard your prayers and gave us an abundance of stuff so we could have the joy of sharing it with you. He's the only one you need to thank."

"I know. But we can thank you for being willing to do God's work. It's such a huge blessing to us." I hugged George again and walked outside with him. He slid into the driver's seat and was off on his forty-five-minute ride back to the children's home.

As I stuffed the last groceries into our now-filled cupboard I laughed and cried, sang and prayed. I thanked God for our loving friends who understood the joy of selfless living expressed in their Christmas giving. Because God blessed them, they generously blessed us.

15. A Chilly Christmas

Marty Prudhomme

LIKE MOST CHILDREN, I HAD NO WORRIES ABOUT THE future. Then my dad lost his job in the spring of 1956. We were forced to move out of our comfortable house—the only home I'd ever known—and into a small rental place. My brother, George, and I had to change schools, leave our friends, and move to a street where no other children lived.

I have no idea how the move affected my parents or how worried they must have been. Even though my mother called it the cracker-box house, she tried to make the best of the situation.

Our little house had only two bedrooms, which meant George and I had to share a room. My brother and I argued about almost everything; he was my archenemy, and I was the little pest who drove him crazy. When we fought with each other, the punishment was to be sent to the same room.

When summer came, we sometimes lay on the floor to keep cool. The building was raised on cinder blocks, and through large cracks in the floorboards we watched ants scurry under the house. Ants carrying what looked like tiny crumbs across the dirt into their colony remains one of my most vivid memories.

Winter that year was extremely cold for South Louisiana. There were several freezes, and for weeks the temperatures dropped into the low thirties and high twenties. The cold wind blew through the cracks in the floorboards and made strange whistling sounds. Even using a wall heater, we constantly felt chilly. George and I came down with colds that turned into pneumonia. Trying to keep us warm, Mom kept us tucked into bed under piles of blankets. George and I became comrades in misery, sick through the entire Christmas holidays.

Mom also became ill and things looked bleak. It was Christmas and, to me, Christmas was about toys, Christmas trees, and big dinners. Lying in bed, I imagined a new baby doll and the typical toys. I wrote my Christmas list and made sure that my parents saw it.

Dad came home one evening with good news. He had found a job and we would soon be able to move into a larger house. We were excited until he told us, "My first paycheck goes to pay the doctor's bill for you kids." Then he said, "That means there will be no money for gifts."

I understood, even though his words didn't make me forget about gifts.

"Everything is going to be all right," he said, and smiled. "Jesus is the real reason we celebrate and give gifts to one another."

"He's the greatest gift of all sent from heaven," Mom added. "If we celebrate because it is Jesus' birthday we'll find special joy in our hearts that only God could give to us."

I smiled despite the fact that I wouldn't get at least one doll for Christmas.

"We may be poor," Dad said, and his voice cracked, "but Jesus first came to the shepherds who were the poorest people in the land."

George and I smiled as our parents hugged us.

"It's going to be all right," I said, and I wanted to believe my own words.

Christmas Day, because of the cold, all four of us huddled in one bed. God's presence filled the little windy house, bringing peace and a deep sense of joy as only He could bring. I didn't think about gifts but felt warmth in my heart knowing I was loved by our parents and loved by the Jesus of Christmas. For the first time, I understood what it meant to have peace on earth and that His love was the greatest gift we could receive.

To our surprise, Mom said, "We don't have any money, but we wanted to do something for you."

"We bought both of you one gift," Dad said.

George received an Erector set.

After I unwrapped a baby doll, I squealed in delight. "Just the one I dreamed about!" She looked like a newborn wearing a delicate long christening dress. I adored her instantly. The tag on her sleeve said her name was Little Love. "She's the most beautiful doll I've ever seen!" I yelled.

More than fifty years later Little Love sits on my bedroom chair. She's slightly faded and a bit tattered, but she's still deeply loved because she's a lasting reminder to me of that very special Christmas when Jesus came to our house.

Since Christmas of 1956, I haven't thought of Christmas as only a time to give and receive gifts. It's a time of love and appreciation for the good things we already have.

It may have been our poorest Christmas, but I remember it as my best Christmas ever.

16. A Father's Love

JoAnn A. Grote

MY THREE BROTHERS AND I PLAYED WITH OUR NEW TOYS until we could hardly keep our eyes open. Reluctantly, we started upstairs to bed.

My parents' home, built in the early 1900s, had a lovely open staircase. Despite my parents' warnings, I regularly played on that staircase. I crawled over the banister and climbed up and down the small step ends beyond the railing.

Even in my holiday exhaustion, and still wearing my satin dress and black patent-leather shoes, as usual I climbed over the banister. This time, perhaps too tired to be careful, I slipped and fell. My forehead struck the uncarpeted edge of the bottom step.

My parents told me I was knocked unconscious. When I awakened in my mother's arms seconds later, I began bawling. Not only did my head ache unbearably, but I had a large, tender lump also.

Sitting on my mother's lap, I sobbed uncontrollably as only a five-year-old can. A cold, wet cloth against my throbbing head drenched the blond curls I'd been so proud of during the holiday evening.

Apparently everyone in the house had gathered around, expressing concern, but nobody was sure what to do for me. Someone put the new doll I had received hours earlier in my lap. I held her tightly; my tears dripped on her face and spotted her navy-blue dress with the wide white collar. Within a short time I calmed down and lay there sniffling.

My anxious parents wondered how they could they keep me awake until they were certain I wouldn't lapse into unconsciousness again.

"Why don't you get the other gift?" my mother asked my father.

A short time later my father handed me a present. It didn't occur to me to wonder at the sudden appearance of a beautifully wrapped present hours after we'd received all our gifts. The box was so large that I had to crawl off my mother's lap to open it.

Inside lay another doll—a bride doll, dressed in a lovely white lace dress and veil. The pearl-like drop earrings matched her necklace. The brunette bride stood almost as tall as I was.

Years later, when the doll was no longer beautiful, the gift brought me even greater joy when my mother told me the story behind it.

My mother did the usual Christmas tasks of writing cards, baking, decorating, and purchasing gifts. My father, the owner of a small business, worked days, evenings, and weekends. He was a generous man, but he could spare little time to help with Christmas preparations. And, like many men of his time, he didn't often express his love in words.

The Christmas I tumbled from the staircase, Mother had purchased the Christmas gifts and among them she bought me a doll. Unknown to her, my busy, hardworking father also bought me a doll.

Once they realized that both of them had bought a doll, they agreed to put one aside for my birthday.

Still dearer is a memory of a Christmas years later when I was a senior in high school and seemed to argue with my parents over everything. I wasn't easy to live with; I'm sure I wasn't an easy person to love.

For Christmas that year I received a hair dryer with a huge robin-egg-blue bonnet. As a teenager before the days of blow-dry hairstyles, I spent untold hours under that blue dryer bonnet, hoping by some miracle to make my hair look like those of the girls in the magazines I read.

That dryer came from my father, who had seen the hair dryer in the local hardware store. Through that Christmas gift, his heart once again reached out wordlessly to me in love. He wasn't good with affectionate words, but his unexpected gifts never allowed me to doubt his love.

At Christmas I'm reminded that another Father chose to express His love through a gift. His gift was more magnificent than dolls or hair dryers. Down through the ages, the incredible gift of His Son assures us of a heavenly Father's unfailing love.

17. A New Beginning

Ron Geelan

CHRISTINE REMOVED THE TOP OF THE GIFT BOX AND GENTLY pushed the tissue paper aside. Her eyes widened. She gasped and threw herself back into the chair. My wife covered her mouth and started sobbing. I bent down to embrace her.

I began to cry, too.

"What's wrong?" our son, Patrick, asked.

"Why are you crying?" our daughter, Erin, leaned forward and asked.

They must have realized that our tears weren't from pain or anger—the kind of crying they had heard so many other nights in our house.

"What's in the box?" Patrick asked.

"Nothing, sweetie." Christine put the top back on the box and wiped away her tears.

"None of your business," I said, and winked.

"Come on, Mom, tell us what's in the box," Erin begged.

Christine stared at me and I nodded.

She motioned for the children to sit beside her next to the tree. Silently she reopened the box and removed the tissue paper. She held up an ordinary piece of lined notebook paper. It was dingy and yellow from age. The words on the paper were in her handwriting.

"Your mother gave me that as a gift fifteen years ago," I said.

"Gross." Patrick pointed to the severely wrinkled paper, covered by tape.

"It looks like someone tore it up," Erin said, "and taped it back together."

"That's exactly right," I replied.

Christine began to cry again, so she pointed to the words at the top of the page: "My Certain Someone."

Patrick shrugged and Erin stared as they waited for an explanation.

"I wrote these poems for your father when we were in college to show him how much I loved him." Christine lifted the paper out of the box to reveal another poem underneath. It was also stained and covered in tape. "Your father cherished these poems." She smiled at me. "He is more sensitive than you may realize."

"Yeah, right," Erin said, and laughed.

"These poems have always been my most prized possession," I said.

"So why are they all torn up?" Patrick asked.

"Because I let my anger get the best of me."

"Your father and I were—and still are—very much in love," Christine said. "But as I'm sure you both know, we've had a tough time lately."

"We know, Mom," Erin said.

"We've heard you," our son added.

Something in Christine's voice told me it was time to be honest with the children about the fighting they had heard in the recent past and to reassure them about the future.

"You know, kids, I have been unhappy for a while now," I said. "I hate my job. And I don't like living in this part of the country." I walked over to the window and stared at lightly falling snow.

The flakes felt peaceful and hypnotic. "I blamed your mother for my unhappiness because she insisted we move here so we could be closer to her family."

The children both knew that much.

"We started to argue—mostly over little things. Each time it seemed to get worse." I looked at both my kids and said, "After you kids went to bed on Thanksgiving, we had our worst fight ever."

"That was when your father tore my poems to shreds right in front of me." With her handkerchief Christine dried her eyes. "He threw the pieces into the garbage and stormed out. I wasn't sure if I would ever see him again. I was positive I'd never see these poems again."

"So what happened?" Erin asked.

"After a long walk and a lot of soul-searching, I came home late that night when everyone was asleep," I said. "I had been wrong. Worse, I had destroyed something valuable—not just the paper, but . . ." I faltered before I said, "I almost ruined our marriage."

The others waited until I was ready to speak again.

"I picked every single piece of paper out of the garbage and taped the poems back together."

"You did a good job," Christine said, holding the paper up to the light of the Christmas tree. "But why did you wait until today to give them to me?"

I walked over to the Christmas tree and stared up at the angel perched on top. Then I turned to *my* angel, who was being comforted by our two children. I sat down on the floor facing her and took her hand as I struggled for the right words.

"After I rushed out of here, I walked aimlessly and stopped only when I reached the center of town on Main Street. I stood in front of the nativity scene inside the park."

"You went that far?" Christine said. "That has to be at least five miles from here."

"I had a lot to think about," I said. "As I stared at the manger, I realized how much I love you and thanked God for the gift of you every night. I began to wonder how I went from thanking God for bringing you into my life to blaming you for all my unhappiness."

Christine squeezed my hand gently while I paused to collect myself.

"As I stood in front of the crèche, I closed my eyes and re-membered many wonderful times we shared, and unconsciously I began to recite your poems. The words touched me even more than the first time I had heard you recite them."

I stopped, unable to continue for a few seconds. My kids sat quietly.

After a few minutes I told them that the longer I stood in front of the nativity scene, the worse I felt. "I had been wrong— totally wrong—and I knew it. I ran all the way home. Once I was back inside the house, I picked up every piece of paper."

"But you never said anything to me," Christine said.

I shook my head. "I was too ashamed. After I finished tap-ing the poems back together, something inside me told me to save them until Christmas morning. I wasn't sure why, but it felt right." I smiled at her and said, "I'm sorry—"

"Maybe you saved it until today because that's when Jesus was born and brought a new beginning into the world," my wife said. "I think it is time for our new beginning."

That happened four years ago. It was a new beginning for us, just as the first gift of Christmas provided a new beginning for all humanity.

18. A Diamond Through the Rough

Patrick Burns

DURING THE LATE 1970S AND EARLY 1980S MY DAD PROSPERED. He worked in Chicago's commodities market as the floor manager for a major trading company. His position paid well with good benefits, but over time, ambition tugged at Dad.

He began to ask himself, *Why am I making millions for a big corporation when I could do exactly the same thing for myself?*

Eventually he stopped asking himself that question and acted on his gut instinct. After nearly two decades, he left the company, purchased his own floor membership at Chicago's Board of Trade, and started trading independently. After a slow start the first year, my dad rode the wave of the bull markets in the late seventies.

Within months, our average middle-class American household seemed to have an inexhaustible supply of cash. The late seventies and early eighties were a time of prosperity for my family.

Then things changed, the markets skidded, and so did my father. He made a number of bad trades and trusted the wrong individuals. The results of those unwise decisions began to chip away at my father's easily acquired wealth. The mid-1980s turned into years of hardship and heartache.

I didn't understand what had happened. Why were my parents liquidating assets such as our RV and summer home? Why had the bank repossessed my mom's Cadillac? How could it be that my father, the self-made millionaire to whom the cost of anything was no concern, couldn't pay the phone bill?

"You're too young to understand," Mom said when I asked. "Maybe someday we can explain it to you. We don't want you worrying about this."

"It's too complicated to explain," Dad said. "It's for your own good."

The seemingly patronizing words of my parents *for your own good* frustrated and angered me. Their words didn't satisfy me. Even though I said, "What happens to you affects me as well," they refused to say more.

The money that had once rushed in now quickly evaporated. Dad sold his membership to the Chicago Board of Trade at a big loss. Like a vanquished gambler leaving the casino with little more than the shirt on his back, Dad was through with that world. He tried to recover and recoup the huge financial losses, but nothing improved. He eventually admitted defeat and said he wouldn't ever be able to rebuild his vanished fortune.

✳ ✳ ✳

In the summer of 1985, when we thought things couldn't get worse, my older brother Billy died in an automobile accident. One day Billy was with us and so full of life—the one family optimist who believed our situation would improve—and then he was gone forever.

Despite our painful loss, we held on even though our financial situation continued to worsen. The cost of Billy's funeral further exacerbated our financial burdens. We were in such bad shape that we couldn't afford a headstone and buried Billy in an unmarked grave.

During the prosperous years, Christmastime had been a high point for our family. Even during our years of hardship, Mom and Dad had found enough money to make sure they filled our Christmas wish lists. In late autumn of the year we lost the house, my mother warned me, "Christmas will be different this year."

"We're officially broke," Dad said.

"This year there won't be any gifts under the tree," Mom added.

This was disappointing but not surprising. By then I had grown up enough to understand some of the turmoil Dad faced. I wondered how they'd survived for so many years.

Despite the deflating news, I tried to look forward to the holidays—even if it meant I wouldn't have a stack of toys and video games (which I probably didn't deserve anyway). To my surprise, the sting of not being spoiled on Christmas wasn't so bad. It was a time to reflect and be thankful for what I did have.

I'd avoided my aunt's living room where the tree was set up in the weeks leading up to Christmas Eve, so I didn't notice the growing stack of gifts. Or maybe I did but assumed they were gifts for my aunt's friends.

On Christmas Eve I took on the duty of handing out gifts to my family.

In the midst of distributing gifts, I realized that this year was just like the previous years: I would receive as many gifts as I had the previous year, perhaps more.

"How can this be?" I asked. "I thought we were broke—"

"We are," Mom said, "but we still want Christmas to be special to you."

"But if you don't have any money—"

"Don't worry about it," Dad said. "Just enjoy your gifts."

I didn't worry, but I wondered. They didn't tell me.

Twenty years later, while I was on vacation in the Florida Keys with my parents, we talked about when I was growing up and what life was like in Chicago.

I don't remember how the subject came up, but Mom mentioned her engagement ring. "After all these years," she said, "I still miss it."

I stared blankly at her left hand. "What do you mean?"

She held out her hand. She was wearing matching rings. As I looked closer, however, I could tell that it wasn't her original wedding set.

"What happened?"

"I wasn't able to get my ring out of hock at the pawnshop—"

"You *pawned* your wedding ring?" I asked. "But when? And *why*?"

"I didn't want to tell you and ruin Christmas for you—"

"What are you talking about?"

"We pawned the rings just before Christmas the year we lost everything," Mom said in a soft but matter-of-fact voice. "My family's enjoyment of the holidays was more important than a material symbol of my marriage."

Impulsively we hugged each other.

✳ ✳ ✳

I still reflect on that selflessness by my mother as one of the most profound acts of kindness and compassion I've ever known.

Her diamond engagement ring had been her most prized material possession, yet she willingly parted with it forever so that her family might be able to enjoy at least one more Christmas as they always had.

When I was a child, my thoughts about the season focused on toys waiting for me under the tree on Christmas Eve. I never thought about what it cost my parents to provide those. Until my mother's statement, I didn't understand what my parents meant when they said they got more enjoyment from giving to others at the holidays than getting gifts themselves.

Now I know. I understand that my parents meant that the spirit of Christmas isn't about receiving, but it's about giving to others. It may mean making personal sacrifices, even in the wake of tragedy, just as God did when He gave the world His only Son.

19. At Home with the Hoppes

Emila Belk

THEY STOOD AT OUR FRONT DOOR—DAD, MOM, FIVE KIDS aged nine months to ten years, their family friend, and a forty-five-pound cat-hating, rambunctious Airedale named Sadie. Snowflakes, whipped by the bitter wind, clung to their hats and coats; raw temperatures froze their exposed cheeks.

Once they walked through our door in late November our holiday season would become drastically different from any we'd ever had. I knew our son and daughter would probably feel as if their space had been invaded and they might resent their dad's decision to invite the family to stay with us.

I had met them briefly once or twice before in a business capacity and, to be honest, my encounters hadn't given me warm feelings. My husband, Steve, knew him more personally through a Bible study they attended together. But we'd never met the rest of the family and didn't know anything about them. That would change quickly, especially now that they would live with us for several weeks.

It began when Steve asked, "Would it be okay if the Hoppes lived with us for a while? Their house deal fell through and they have nowhere to go."

Steve gave enough details to convince me that we couldn't leave a family of seven stranded and homeless in the middle of a blizzard. "I guess we can try to make it work." I didn't like the invasion, but I knew it was the right thing for us to do.

When we had moved into our house a few months earlier, Steve and I agreed that we wanted to use it to help others, if necessary. This was apparently the time it was needed.

We felt blessed to have a big house with four levels of living space. But now, when the opportunity to help others arrived, I was concerned. We hadn't yet made any upgrades to the house. The carpet was old and stained. We didn't have furniture in our living room and had not much elsewhere.

What will they think of us? Where will they sit? Where will they sleep? What will we do with them?

The food issue also concerned me. I didn't have much on hand and didn't have time to buy any before they arrived. It would have been difficult to go out in the midst of a severe Iowa-winter storm anyhow.

What will I feed them?

I wrestled with feelings of inadequacy, but I found peace as I tried to imagine that the Hoppe family struggled even more with all the hardship they faced. They had been uprooted from everything they'd known and had no place to go. They faced an uncertain future because his business had failed. That's hard enough for adults to go through, but for the children it must have been impossible to comprehend.

How do young children understand their father's failed business and having to sell their home? How do young children understand the hope of starting over, only to have the deal on their new house fall through an hour before closing? How do kids grasp that everything they owned was in a storage shed or on the back of a truck? How do young children realize that Christmas would not exist for them that year? How do young children understand that they had no choice but to share a home with strangers?

Steve and I determined that, with God's help, we'd make it a good experience for everyone.

I scrounged through the pantry and grabbed all the noodles—spaghetti, lasagna, linguini, and angel-hair. I figured I could come up with enough ingredients to create some sort of spaghetti sauce to cover the pasta. I threw together our canned, frozen, and fresh vegetables. It didn't matter what they were because they would fill our stomachs. We made garlic toast out of half a loaf of bread.

I apologized for the hodgepodge meal and explained that anything goes at our house. The Hoppes loved it. To them a shelter from the storm, a warm welcome, hot food, and permission to feel "at home" was what they needed.

We set up an eight-foot rectangular table and folding chairs in our bare living room. We were grateful to have the chairs stored in the garage. There was just enough room for the kids at the living room table and the adults at the nearby dining room table.

This is going to work, I thought. And I prayed.

The Hoppes settled in. The third and fourth levels of the house became their living space. Tom and Donna Hoppe slept in the spare bedroom on the third level. They brought in a crib for the baby. They laid wall-to-wall mattresses in the family room for the rest of their kids and set up a twin bed in the fourth level for their friend. We made space in the garage for whatever furniture they didn't bring into the house from their truck. Our lack of furniture worked to their advantage.

I prepared most of the meals. I don't mind cooking, but I dislike cleaning. Donna didn't mind cleaning, but she disliked cooking. We made an excellent team.

We baked Christmas cookies and decorated the house together. Donna made beautiful raffia bows to hang on the doorposts and ribbon bows for the tree. Years later, I still use many of those Christmas bows.

On Christmas Day our family planned to exchange small gifts with the Hoppe family, but on Christmas Eve Steve and I created another Christmas memory for our son and daughter by opening presents in our bedroom among the mounds of dirty laundry. We didn't want the Hoppe children to feel as if they were missing out.

It might not always have been a good experience for everyone, but it worked. And it worked well.

Our kids had conflicts and clashes. Our cat and the killer dog did, too. We tried to protect the cat by keeping her confined in the workshop on the fourth level, but occasionally she escaped and chaos broke loose. A few times we had to remove her body from Sadie's mouth. And there was the morning we discovered piles of puke throughout the house after Sadie ate a basketful of Butterfinger chocolate bars the night before. But, in retrospect, those incidents only added to the fun memories of the first Christmas in our new house, the one we shared with the Hoppes.

The Christmas we opened our hearts and home to the Hoppes was a memorable one for us. We learned that it's possible to be grateful for lack of furniture and for old, stained carpet.

Most of all, we learned that we can and will be blessed when we willingly offer whatever gifts we have to those in need.

20. Christmas Vision

Jane Owen

When I opened the door, my seventy-nine-year-old neighbor stood in front of me. He had a fresh, jagged cut above his left eye.

"What happened?"

"It's a bit of a story," Sam said as he leaned on his cane.

"Come inside." I took his arm and led him into the house.

He eased his lean body into a nearby chair. "I was walking to the bus stop. I wanted to do some Christmas shopping. I tripped on the sidewalk and went down."

"How did you get up?" I stared at the ugly gash. "Did someone help you?"

He shook his head slowly. "Three or four cars whizzed by, but no one stopped."

"That's outrageous!"

"It was a struggle," he said. "It took a few tries, but I made it. I couldn't just lie there."

I leaned close and studied his wound. "I think you're just short of needing stitches."

He fumbled inside his pocket. "Here's my problem." His hands shook a little as he showed me the remains of his glasses. The lenses were scratched and no optician would be able to straighten out the plastic frames.

"You hit that cement hard."

"I know."

We talked for a few more minutes while I cleaned and bandaged his wound. He didn't try to gain my pity but remained quite matter-of-fact about his situation.

"I'm going to the optician's tomorrow," I said. "Why don't you go with me?"

"I'd like that." He bent forward and stood up. "You're a good neighbor."

"We're good neighbors together."

The next morning at the optician's, I introduced Sam to Georgette, the manager. Her gaze lingered on his injury, but she smiled and asked, "How may I help you?"

"I fell yesterday and busted these." He opened a paper bag that contained the broken pieces. "Think you could fix them?"

She glanced from the contents to me and back to Sam. "Perhaps we can buffer out the lenses and fit them into new frames. Sit here. I'll see what I can find."

After a few moments, she returned with scratch-free lenses. She held up two frames. "I found these, but the dimensions don't match. Your lenses are too large for this one and too small for the other."

"What should I do?"

"When was your vision last checked?"

"I don't remember—it's been a while."

"Would you be willing to see our optometrist?"

"I think I should." He turned to me. "Do you have time to wait?"

"Of course I do."

He turned to Georgette. "First, we better talk about the cost.

I can pay—installments would be better for me. I'll sign any papers necessary."

"Don't worry about that," she replied. "We'll work out the details."

Silently I prayed for Sam. I knew the charges for new frames and the doctor's visit were beyond his means. *Lord, how can I pay his fees without his knowing?*

Sam's eye exam showed he needed a stronger prescription. After the exam, Georgette showed him several frames. "Let's see which of these you like best, sweetheart."

He nudged me and grinned at her affectionate term. He tried on each frame and appraised himself in a side mirror. "It's hard to choose. What do you suggest?" he asked Georgette.

"Which is most comfortable?"

"These expandable, hinged ones feel the best."

Georgette double-checked the measurements and flashed a smile. "We'll have them ready for you in an hour."

Leaving the store with me, he said, "She is the most caring professional person I've met."

"I couldn't agree more," I said, but my mind still raced on as I tried to figure out how I could pay for his glasses without offending him. He was a strong, independent man.

Christmas music filtered through the mall as we joined the stream of shoppers. We rested briefly near the festive Christmas tree where a jolly Santa entertained wide-eyed children eagerly reciting their wishes. Sam's eyes sparkled along with the lights and tinsel. "Those sweet children do your heart good, don't they?"

"That they do."

"As a youngster in the back reaches of Idaho, I never had a Christmas tree," Sam said.

"Why not?" I asked.

He pressed his lips together. "We were poor folks who treated December 25 like any other cold winter's day."

I thought he would continue, but giggling children caught our attention. Sam and I laughed to see twin girls tugging at Santa's beard.

Our spirits were light as we returned to the eye center. "We're ready for you," Georgette said.

Sam tried on his new glasses and viewed himself from different angles in the mirror. "These fit better than any glasses I've ever had."

Georgette put away her tools.

"You have a sale," Sam said. "What do I need to sign?"

I made a feeble attempt to catch Georgette's eye. *Dear Lord, what should I do?*

She reached over and placed her hands on his. "Merry Christmas, Sam."

"And to you, too," he said, and chuckled. "Now about my payments. Could they begin in January?"

Her gaze never wavered. "Merry Christmas," she repeated. "It was my pleasure to help you."

I understood and reached for a Kleenex.

Sam's eyes searched her face. "I must owe you something."

"I don't think you do."

I smiled at Georgette and dabbed my eyes.

"I don't owe you *anything*? Nothing?"

"That's right," she said.

His blue eyes widened. "I don't know what to say, but thank you!"

"You're quite welcome. Merry Christmas."

As we left, he hesitated. "Did she just *give* me these glasses?"

"Yes, she did."

We had witnessed God's love in action, without any interference from me.

Sam turned around and stared at Georgette, who was with another customer. "No one ever has done something nice like this for me."

I linked my arm in his. "I believe Jesus spoke to that dear woman's heart, and because of her love for Jesus, she wanted to bless you."

"I am blessed! That little gal has opened my eyes to the true spirit of Christmas. I'll never forget her kindness."

"Nor will I, Sam. Nor will I."

21. Karen's Timely Gift

Shawnelle Eliasen

"I'M ABOUT FORTY-FIVE SECONDS FROM A MELTDOWN," I SAID.

My husband, Lonny, stared at me.

"I'm serious. I'm so pressured for time. If we add one more thing to our calendar, I'll sit down and cry."

We stood in the toy store, laboring over which plastic pirate ship our two-year-old would like the most.

"Where's your joy?" Lonny asked. "It's Christmas."

"I don't have time for joy," I said. "I've been running around like an insane woman. I have to assemble fifty graham cracker gingerbread houses for our homeschool co-op by Friday. I haven't written one Christmas letter. The kids haven't had their Christmas pictures taken, and I have to find gifts for both our mothers." I picked up a box and poked my finger at a pirate with a sword. "Now, do you think this is too scary or not?" I didn't add the words, but I think Lonny caught my mood, "We're running late with our shopping, and we need to get going."

"Can't you just relax and enjoy our time together?" Lonny asked.

"I'd love to, but there's still too much to do." I plunked the ship into the bottom of our cart and wheeled to the front of the store. As we waited in the December-long line, I pulled up the sleeve of my winter coat to check my watch.

We continued to shop that evening. With each stop, I took a black Sharpie and marked a line through an item on our list. We did what we planned to do, but we didn't have much fun. I reasoned that we'd have some fun in January, after the wild Christmas rush.

Every square on our family calendar was full, and we would bolt from one holiday event to another. I was tired. My husband, even if he wouldn't admit it, was tired. I felt stressed out, wishing Christmas were over.

Our five boys were tired, too. All of the activities were good, but it felt like too much of a good thing.

The next day after our shopping trip, I creamed butter and sugar in my big mixing bowl and thought of all the things I had scheduled. We had a holiday concert to attend that night, and I needed to bake two dozen cookies for the fellowship afterward. My boys swarmed around my feet.

"Can't you read us a story?" one son asked.

"Or sit down with us and watch a Christmas movie together?" another asked.

"I'd love to do it, but I have to get those cookies done." I cracked eggs against the side of my bowl and looked at my boys. "You'll have to keep busy for a few minutes," I said.

They looked at me with sad eyes.

"Maybe you could look through the box of Christmas books."

Just then the phone rang and I stretched for the telephone receiver and wedged it between my shoulder and chin. "Hello," I said as I scooped sugar from the canister.

It was my friend Karen and she asked how I was.

"Crazy busy." I dipped a teaspoon into the baking soda.

" 'Tis the season," she said. "Hey, can I bring your Christmas gift over this afternoon?"

"I'm pretty full today," I said. I mentally scrolled through the day's commitments. Cookies for concert. Homeschool lessons. Quick dinner. Church by seven. I loved Karen and she and I were longtime friends, but I didn't want to squeeze one more thing into the day's activities. "How about later in the week?"

"Tell you what. I'll just drop your gift by. It'll take only a few minutes."

"I don't have your gift yet," I said.

"It's okay. Later this afternoon?"

I decided to give in. "Four o'clock?"

"See you then," she said.

I looked forward to seeing my friend, but my stress increased even more. I hoped I hadn't cut things too close. The boys needed dark socks for the concert, and I hadn't had time to think about the mounds of dirty laundry that now lived in the washroom.

The rest of the day was one of full-scale activity. When Karen's van pulled into the driveway, I was shocked. *Four o'clock already?* I arranged a few of the fresh cookies on a plate and filled the teapot. "Boys," I called, "Miss Karen is here." I waited at the back door. When Karen didn't come down the walk, I pulled the curtain back and peered out the frosty window. I turned to stare at the still-ticking clock. It was 4:03.

Finally Karen got out of her van and pulled out her guitar case. She'd been taking lessons, but why was she bringing her guitar to my house? She shut the van door and started down the walkway.

"What are you doing?" I asked after I opened the door for my friend.

"I brought your Christmas present."

"Your guitar?"

"No, I brought you a song." She handed me the cold, smooth case while she tugged off her coat.

A few minutes later, the boys and I sat on the living room sofa. It was now 4:09 and I hoped it wouldn't take long.

The older brothers held the younger ones, and the baby lay in my arms. Despite the time pressure, it felt good to sit. It felt even better to have my boys surround me.

"I'm a beginner, so I'll need grace." Karen sat on the wing chair. "I've never done this before."

Karen's fingers began to move over the strings of the guitar. Sweet, gentle music filled the room. The tune was a familiar carol, "God Rest Ye Merry, Gentlemen." The sound was clear and pure, and it captivated five boys and their mama.

Then Karen began to sing: "God rest ye merry, gentlemen. Let nothing you dismay. Remember Christ the Savior was born on Christmas Day . . ."

I gazed at my young sons. Their blond heads tipped together in stillness and peace. I glanced at my friend who smiled as she sang. Then I closed my eyes. The clock disappeared. The calendar vanished. The cookies and socks and all the other pressures were pushed from my mind.

I joined my friend in singing, "Remember Christ the Savior was born on Christmas Day . . ."

Karen played for a few more minutes. When she was finished, she hugged me.

"Thank you," I said softly.

Karen's song reminded me of the real meaning of Christmas. She gave me a moment to rest—a forced rest—and to hold my sons close. Her gift carried me through the rest of the day and even the rest of the season. I worked through the tasks with renewed focus. I deleted a few minor events from the calendar. My boys and I took time to snuggle on the couch while I read to them about Christmas and we watched old holiday movies.

I took time to reflect on the blessings God brought to my life. Like my friend Karen and her timely gift.

22. Mama's Wish

Chris Griffin

THE NIGHT AIR WAS COLD AND CLEAR AS WE PREPARED FOR dinner with my brother Ron and with Mama. With Christmas only a few weeks away, their trip from Florida to Maryland greatly added to our holiday excitement. I had not seen Mama for a couple of years, and with her declining health I was grateful for the opportunity to have time with her.

As we sat talking, the faint sound of sirens in the background brought loud, piercing screams all through our neighborhood in Woodlawn, Maryland. I stared out the window as fire engines and emergency vehicles came closer.

"I wonder whose house is on fire," I said. A fire is always terrible, but just before Christmas seemed so much worse.

"They're on our street!" my wife said.

My wife and I and my mother ran outside and watched as the caravan of emergency vehicles rolled slowly down our street. We waited to see at which house they would stop with their spotlights aimed into the sky and red lights flashing. Just then a voice from a loudspeaker greeted us with, "Merry Christmas, Merry Christmas! Ho! Ho! Ho!" It came from Santa Claus riding atop the bright red ladder truck of Woodlawn's fire department.

My mother's face beamed as she waved wildly and laughed excitedly. I stared at her and was thankful for her presence with us. She had already suffered several ministrokes. She was short and had put on her long black coat with its fake fur collar. In the coat and with her hair curled tight, she looked more like a child than the elderly person she had become.

My wife and I yelled in relief and excitement. I've never been a fan of the big guy. He gets too much credit and steals the show from the main character, but I couldn't help myself. It just came over me. There's something about a lit-up red ladder truck with Santa sitting on top that makes me smile and enjoy the moment.

We waited while the fire truck rolled slowly along, making occasional stops for Santa to throw candy onto the sidewalks. Children rushed madly for the candy and a few adults reached for candy that bounced into the grass.

For a few minutes, it was as if we were in a different world; life stood still and we were kids again, when there came a wonderful pause. There was Santa, with the streetlight as his backdrop, sitting atop the fire truck as it lit up the night with its spotlights.

"Wouldn't it be wonderful if it snowed right now?" Mama said.

Just then something even more magical happened. Standing in the bright lights of the truck, which was now directly in front of us, we saw them. First there was only one or two flakes, and then another floated slowly past the streetlight. Within minutes the spotlighted night filled with snowflakes.

Mama's wish had come true.

As we looked up in amazement, Santa threw back his head while holding out his arms shouting, "Ho, ho, ho!"

Stunned, I turned to Mama, aware that tears in her eyes reflected the bright lights as the fire truck rolled onward.

As the parade of sirens and lights continued down the street, as if on cue the falling snow ceased as quickly as it had begun. Once again the sky was clear, and there was nothing more than a few wet spots on our coats to prove it had snowed on that clear night.

My wife and I stared at each other in disbelief and I asked, "What's the possibility that it would begin to snow at the very second Mama made her wish and stop as soon as the truck rolled on?"

Mama sighed as though she had just lived the most wondrous moment of her life. For me, it was a moment I can't forget—don't want to forget. I can say only that I was caught up in the miraculous mood of Christmas as I stood next to my beloved mother.

A few more Christmases came for Mama, but I could tell she had lost the strength and the zeal to participate as she once had. Her strokes increased in intensity and frequency. She often forgot who we were and couldn't recognize or name her grandchildren.

On November 8, 2005, Mama joined Dad in eternity.

As I think about Christmas and about Mama, I'll never forget the night we stood in that snowfall, waving at Santa, and God granted her wish. Why He chose that moment to show her His gentle love I will never understand, but that is what makes Him God.

While we often struggle over the true meaning of Christmas, God waits for just one special moment, if that is all we allow Him, to show us He is among us.

23. When PopPop Sang

Lauren Yarger

WHEN MY GRANDPARENTS MARRIED DURING THE GREAT Depression, it wasn't for love. Times were tough, they liked each other, and that seemed enough. They struggled to live and prosper and to raise a family. They also struggled with each other.

During the early years of their life together my grandfather made colossal mistakes, and Grandma never forgave him. In her eyes, he'd lost all her respect for him as a husband and as a man. By the time I was born it was common for Grandma to express those negative feelings for PopPop (as I called him) to anyone who would listen.

Grandma, whom I loved dearly and whom I take after in many ways, was domineering and expected everyone to do exactly as she said. I understand that. She had come from a home with a strict father who tolerated no disobedience. Her parents barely knew each other when they married. Family lore says that on the way to the ceremony at the Town Hall my great-grandmother asked her husband-to-be, "What is your first name?" True or not, they hardly provided a model of a healthy marriage.

I know only that Grandma didn't respect PopPop, so she didn't think anyone else should, either, and her public criticism of him often went unchallenged. I never thought about it much, perhaps because I had heard the negative comments all my life. That was just how my grandparents were and it never occurred to me that PopPop minded. He didn't argue or defend himself.

Once I asked Grandma, "If he's so awful why didn't you divorce PopPop a long time ago?"

"I don't *hate* PopPop," she said. "We live in the same house. I'm fond of him."

It wasn't exactly a stunning testimony for marriage.

The only time I spent time alone with PopPop was during baseball season. I was an obsessed New York Mets fan, and I watched or listened to every game. PopPop also was a baseball fan. He'd gone to Florida for many years for spring training and I still had pictures of him with Babe Ruth, Lefty Gomez, and other heroes of that era. PopPop and I often watched a Mets game together during the summer weekends I spent at my grandparents' house. He usually had to leave before the end of the game to get to his job. He worked the night shift, which according to Grandma was a blessing because that meant they didn't need to see much of each other. He slept during the day.

Grandma criticized PopPop for watching too much baseball, but when I became a fanatic she stopped that part of her complaining. I assumed it was because the criticism would have touched me because I watched even more than he did. And in her eyes, I could do no wrong.

At Christmas, our big family problem was always this question: "What do we buy for PopPop?"

"What does he need?" I asked Grandma year after year.

Every year I received the same answer: "He doesn't need anything."

So every year, I bought him candy and cookies because I knew he liked them. Grandma bought him underwear.

Christmas at Grandma's was a magical time for me. We gathered to exchange gifts, give PopPop his tins of cookies and candy, and sit down to our hot pastrami dinner. Grandma said the best Jewish deli in New Jersey was around the corner from her house, and they weren't closed on Christmas. So we feasted on their pastrami and prized potato salad instead of the traditional ham or turkey.

One year, we gathered in the kitchen, but PopPop had stayed in the living room watching television. The local TV station traditionally showed a scene of logs burning in a fireplace while they played Christmas music.

Just then, above the talk and laughter in the kitchen, I heard the most beautiful tenor singing "The First Noel." Wondering which opera star they were featuring on the "Yule Log" program, I went into the living room. It was PopPop sitting in the chair singing along with the music.

"I didn't know you could sing," I said at the end of the song when he rose to join the rest of the family in the kitchen.

He looked straight at me and said in his soft-spoken voice, "There are a lot of things about me you don't know."

I stood there and felt the cracking of a stone-cold heart. He was right: I didn't know anything about him. I'd never been interested or tried to get to know him. Just as suddenly, it came to me that the reason I never knew what to get him for Christmas year after year was because I didn't know *him* year after year.

That man had been a part of my life for many years, yet I couldn't have told anyone more than a few facts about him. What little I did know I had learned from someone else and not from him.

I asked God to guide my heart and to give me a chance to know PopPop better.

Spending time with him wasn't easy, because by then I had moved out of state and visits were infrequent and brief, but I talked to him occasionally on the phone.

The next Christmas, I decided to try to make him candy. I still didn't know what to get him, but at least I could personalize it to let PopPop know he was special to me. It wasn't an artistic endeavor and the meringue-covered chocolate kisses that looked so delicate and tempting in the recipe book resembled lumpy, dirty golf balls. I packaged them up with a sigh and headed there for Christmas.

When PopPop opened his package, family members laughed and made jokes about the less-than-tempting creations within.

"I've never made candy before," I protested.

"You made these?" PopPop asked.

"Yes," I answered embarrassedly.

"You *made* these for me?" he asked again with tears in his eyes. "I love them," he said before he kissed me.

I never could have guessed that such a small act of kindness could mean so much.

Some years later, the Mets finally played in the World Series. PopPop and I still chatted a lot about the games, and when the Mets won the seventh game I could hardly wait to get on the phone the next day to whoop it up with PopPop. As I dialed the number, I knew my heart really had changed since that Christmas when he sang. I chuckled as I realized that I was calling him this time, not my grandmother.

When Grandma answered the phone, she told me PopPop had died in his sleep the night before. We didn't get to celebrate the championship together, but I knew that I had won a victory much more important. Every time I hear "The First Noel," it is a reminder of God's love, born in a lowly manger. He doesn't take anyone for granted and neither should I.

24. A Mysterious Christmas Gift

Ada Brownell

A BLIZZARD BLEW INTO COLORADO ON CHRISTMAS EVE, chilling our bodies; our emotions had already been frozen because our daughter Carolyn had been diagnosed with Burkitt's lymphoma.

The day after Thanksgiving, instead of coming home for the holidays in Colorado with her husband, she was fighting for her life in California.

Carolyn and her husband, Michael, had made Amtrak reservations months before for their expected Christmas trip. We were excited that we would all be together. That was before the diagnosis.

They canceled the trip and that saddened us.

A big turkey sat in the refrigerator, ready for the oven. The other nine of us planned to gather at our home. Pumpkin and apple crumb pies, Aunt Daisy's pudding, dressing mix, vegetables, and salads were ready to go.

Our oldest son, Gary, and his wife, Janice, and their two children lived in Denver. They planned to leave Christmas morning and drive to our house in Pueblo, about one hundred miles away.

In the early morning, I stood at the window, my chest heavy, almost beyond feeling. Huge snowflakes fell from the skies as if the clouds had been thrown into a grinder. City streets glistened with ice while yellow city trucks rumbled by, scraping the roads and dumping sand. Minutes later I couldn't see where the blade had plowed or the sand had been spread.

Just as the family started to stir, the phone rang.

"We can't come," Janice said. "We had to take Justin to the emergency room last night. He has the croup."

Without giving it serious thought, impulsively I said, "Then we'll pack up the gifts, the food, and come to your house."

Gary and Janice were shocked but delighted.

"Besides, we need this day together," I said. I told her how heavy my heart was for Carolyn. "And after we're there, we can call her and talk to her."

My husband, who ordinarily hates snowy travel, agreed we'd go.

"We're going to Denver," I announced to Carolyn's two sisters and her other brother. "Pack up everything."

Within a short time we packed suitcases, the food, and Christmas presents and loaded everything into the van. We had good snow tires. But even more, we're a praying family and we prayed for God to give us a safe journey over the treacherous highways.

I felt calm about going. Vehicles in the median and along each side of I-25 made the perils of the slippery interstate obvious. We counted more than seventy abandoned vehicles along the road. But we made the trip without any problems.

When we arrived, Gary was still shoveling the deep snow from his long driveway. His joyous smile made me realize how pleased he felt to see us.

Once we were inside, Janice, their daughter, Melissa, and little Justin were excited that we had come.

The children placed the gifts under the tree while we adults carried the food into the kitchen. Within minutes cooking aromas permeated the house.

While Janice and I took over the cooking, Dad and Gary found and unpacked the phones and looked for an already-installed wall phone jack that would work so we could call Carolyn. Gary and his family had moved into the house a few days earlier and ordered phone service. No one had come out yet and they couldn't get a dial tone on any of their phones.

We desperately needed the telephone connection. I felt I absolutely had to talk to my daughter. The house was large, and there were prewired phone jacks in every room, so they kept trying. The year was 1989, before any of us had cell phones. It was the holidays and the Denver area was shrouded in a blizzard. No telephone serviceman would come out that day.

"We found a jack that works!" Dad shouted. They hooked it up and we had a dial tone.

Only a few seconds lapsed before we had Carolyn on the line. We talked more than an hour because all of us wanted a turn. She had a great sense of humor, never lost hope, and sick as she was, she said she enjoyed speaking to each one. Although we never forgot her cancer, there was laughter, happy sharing, love, and prayer.

As I watched the others, I gave thanks to God for Alexander Graham Bell's invention that brought us together, although more than one thousand miles lay between us.

That call may not have been the single most important thing that happened that Christmas, but through the years the memory has stayed alive and made me realize how much God loves us.

Two days after Christmas, a telephone serviceman arrived and connected the phones. Janice thanked him and said, "We had no dial tone. We were able to make just one call—on Christmas Day—but we haven't been able to call anyone since then."

He stared at her and shook his head as if to say, "Impossible."

Before Janice could ask what he meant, he said, "There is no way you talked on the phone—any phone in this house—"

"But we did—"

"Impossible. You had no connection."

He didn't believe her, and apparently Ma Bell didn't, either.

Gary and Janice never received a bill for the long-distance call.

✳ ✳ ✳

The call brought so much joy on Christmas Day and we viewed it as a special, loving gift from God. On January 29, a little more than a month after our phone call and two months after the diagnosis, Carolyn's body surrendered to the aggressive form of lymphoma. She went to heaven.

Sometimes we wonder at the mysterious Christmas Day miracle God gave us. It was a special gift and we've always been grateful. Even though we prayed fervently, we didn't receive an answer to our other prayer—healing for Carolyn's body.

After her death, I read the Gospel of John and was especially touched by 11:35, which says Jesus wept after he learned about the death of his dear friend Lazarus. They tell me that's the shortest verse in the English translation. Short or long doesn't matter, but those two words do: *Jesus wept.* He feels our sorrows and understands.

In the years since then, I've understood more fully why Jesus is also called Immanuel. The Hebrew word means "God with us." And he is.

He was so close to us that Christmas Day of 1989. He felt our pain and let us connect with our beloved Carolyn. I continue to thank God for that miracle of love from God.

25. Silent Night, Magical Night

Drienie Hattingh

CHRISTMAS EVE 1999 STANDS OUT IN MY MEMORY AS ONE OF the most memorable and spiritual of all. It was the year my mother, Ralie, visited us from South Africa. For the first time in many years we were together at Christmas.

At midnight the sanctuary was dark and silent inside, and then the words of the age-old song started filling the church.

"Silent night, holy night . . ." I could feel the holiness all around.

"All is calm, all is bright . . ." Outside my window, the world looked beautiful, calm, and bright. A full moon reflected off the freshly fallen snow. The sky, air, and snow looked lovely in a luminous pink glow; it was as bright as day. Even now, the strange phenomenon of that day still amazes me.

Along with my husband, Johan, and our two children, Brenda and Yolandi, and my mother, I attended the midnight Christmas Eve Candlelight Service at Woodbury Lutheran in Woodbury, Minnesota.

A small light flickered in front of the dark sanctuary. Pastor Paul's face glowed in the soft light of the candle. He walked down from the pulpit to the person in the first row. That person held out his candle to Pastor Paul. Then there were two little lights shining in the church filled with a thousand believers.

One by one our candles were lit as our neighbors offered their flames to ignite our candles. I've always had a feeling of closeness to the person who leans over and lights my candle, even if the person is a stranger. For those seconds, with our faces glowing softly in the light of a small flame, I feel as though the person is giving me something precious while lighting my candle.

It fascinated me to see that one small flame from Pastor Paul's candle could light up a whole sanctuary, passed along, one by one. As I sat at the midnight candlelight service holding my candle, I thought this must be how God wants us to light up the world. One by one we need to lean over to our fellow earth dwellers and share the light that was lit in our hearts by another Christian.

In my case my grandmothers and my mother passed it on to me. Since the birth of our children, we have done the same. We passed on the little fragile flame of hope to them, praying that life's struggles wouldn't extinguish it.

Earlier in the service, we had gone forward for communion. As we do in the Lutheran church, I knelt down with Yolandi, Brenda, Johan, and my mother. I felt humbled and my heart filled with gratefulness toward our heavenly Father. I thanked God for His Son, the greatest gift of all. I thanked God for my family and friends spread out across the world. I prayed for divine protection over all of them.

Mother and I stared into each other's smiling eyes. I was so happy to have her sharing this special Christmas Eve service with us. I knew she loved her visit and this new adventure. She enjoyed the snow and the beauty it brought to everyday things. And she was enthralled that Johan and I had found this place to worship in our new land.

She had felt troubled when we left South Africa, but now she knew we had found not only a safe home but also a place to worship.

My thoughts were interrupted and my eyes filled with sudden tears when I heard my daughter Yolandi's strong, sweet seventeen-year-old voice next to me sing, "Sleep in heavenly peace. . . ."

That Christmas Eve of 1999, the last Christmas of the twentieth century, I stood up along with my loved ones, including my dear mother. We raised our lighted candles high in the air and sang the final stanza of "Silent Night."

I felt the Christmas spirit shower down upon us.

26. He Didn't Believe

Woody McKay

THIS IS A STORY MY FATHER TOLD ME MANY YEARS AGO. I want to tell it the way he told me.

It begins with the words of a small boy.

"I don't believe in Santa Claus anymore," my boss's grandson declared. "I think he's a phony."

Startled by the statement, my boss clearly didn't know what to say. He later told me he thought the boy probably heard the older boys at school laugh at anyone who said he believed in Santa Claus: "He doesn't want them to laugh at him and his childish beliefs."

After thinking a few minutes, my boss said to his grandson, "Let's see what happens this Christmas before we come to a conclusion on Santa."

The puzzled boy, used to his grandfather's odd responses, shrugged and walked away. Although the boy probably forgot about his statement of disbelief, my boss didn't. After giving the matter a great deal of thought, he made a decision. With the help of three of his managers, within a week he had a plan.

A Michigan-based circus headed south every winter to continue its operation under warmer weather conditions. Not everyone went because several members of the traveling troupe stayed home to be with their families. One of them was a dwarf, who was also a skilled carpenter and made marionettes for one of the acts. For many Christmases, he carved toys for his children and sold additional ones to stores in the Detroit area.

After my boss learned about the little man, he explained about his grandson. "I'd like to give you a job to become Santa's helper." My boss offered fair compensation for the work.

"I'd like that," the circus man said. "I can earn money and still spend Christmas with my family."

My boss had purchased a cabin in the midst of several acres of forest outside Dearborn, Michigan. That would become the site of the workshop, and he provided all the supplies the carpenter wanted. For several weeks the circus-man carpenter made toys. He was only one man, though, and he couldn't produce enough to have the cabin filled before Christmas.

That wasn't an insurmountable problem for my boss and his managers: They bought enough toys from a local store to fill the shelves.

"Now we need to make you look like an elf," one of the managers said. Someone measured the dwarf, and my boss had a suit made so that it fit the little man perfectly. They also gave him a long, white costume beard so he looked exactly like pictures children had seen of Santa's elves.

"Now all we need is a good snow," one of the managers said.

Nature cooperated. Exactly one week before Christmas Eve, an eight-inch snow covered the woods and provided a white apron around the cabin. Smoke curled from the stone chimney. Reindeer, imported for the occasion, foraged in the underbrush. Food supplies scattered daily in the nearby woods kept them from wandering away.

"Bring my car to the office in thirty minutes," my boss said when he called me. I was his driver and had been for several years. "I want you to take my grandson and me for a ride in the woods."

"Yes, sir, I'll be there."

Until then, I hadn't known about the plan, but I sensed something special was about to happen. I had worked for him long enough to know he often did kind and unexpected things. His voice held a quiet excitement.

I picked up both of them. The boy had no idea where he was going. Despite his questions, his grandfather smiled and said, "Soon. You'll see it soon."

An old logging road led to the log cabin in the woods. Several times I glanced at my boss's face through the rearview mirror, and it seemed as if he smiled the entire forty-five minutes.

The boy seemed genuinely excited. He stared at the snow and the sights. The rugged road mesmerized him as our headlights shone on a road on which no car had driven since the snow. "Will the surprise be soon, Grandpa?" he asked several times.

The old man only smiled.

Despite the rough and rutted road, covered with heavy snow, we were able to reach the cabin with no problems. At the clearing, light from the cabin windows shone outside. A slight breeze caused shadows to dance on the snow. As I opened the doors for my boss and his grandson, the aroma of wood smoke and the crisp air created a perfect setting.

As if on cue, a reindeer wandered to the edge of the clearing to nibble on a few remaining leaves of a bush.

"Look, Granddaddy, a reindeer!" gasped the youngster. "Look, Grandpa. A real reindeer!"

The old man smiled and took the boy's hand. "Wait until you

get inside," he said. He opened the door of the warmed cabin. The red-and-white-suited carpenter was busily making new toys.

For several seconds the wide-eyed grandson stood silent as he surveyed the entire cabin. "Look! Look!" He stared in disbelief. "This is real!"

"Look all around," the pleased granddad said. "Let me know what you like and maybe Santa will bring you one of his toys for Christmas."

My boss led the boy around the cabin as the child squealed in delight at many toys. The tour ended at the carpenter's workbench.

"Are you really Santa's helper? Did you make all these toys?" Those were only two of the dozen questions the boy asked.

The little man knew exactly the answers to give and his face was almost as animated as the child's. As I waited just inside the door, I laughed and smiled along with them. I'd rarely seen my boss have such a great time.

"Time to go," the old man said to the boy.

"Okay," the boy said with disappointment in his voice as they headed toward the door.

"I wish you a very, very Merry Christmas," the old man said.

"Yes! And tell Santa hello and that I've been good," the boy said.

I hardly noticed the chilled air on the return ride. The boy talked about the toys and the reindeer but mostly about Santa's elf. "He was real, Grandpa. A real elf!"

All through dinner that night, the boy talked excitedly about his trip.

"So you believe in Santa Claus?" the old man said.

"Oh yes! Yes!"

The experiment worked, my boss told me. "My grandson has become a believer again in the magic of Christmas."

That's not the end. My boss, a wizened engineer, didn't forget what pleasure the event had brought to his grandson. In subsequent Christmas seasons, hundreds of smiling children journeyed into the woods near Dearborn to discover Santa's workshop. Each one received a hand-carved toy from the short, bearded Santa helper.

The children never knew the name of their benefactor. But of course, I knew. My boss was Henry Ford.

I've sometimes thought the God who brought the first gift of Christmas must have smiled at the joy that Henry Ford brought to children for many years. Even a hardened and worldly-wise engineer can be touched by the true spirit of Christmas.

27. The Christmas Manger Scene

Annmarie B. Tait

MY DAD HADN'T WORKED SINCE OCTOBER OF 1966 BECAUSE of a strike at the steel mill, so when Christmas came there was no money. That had little effect on me as far as Christmas goes. I knew Santa brought the presents, and at nine years old I counted on getting plenty of them. To me it was mere coincidence that the birth of Jesus fell on the same day that Santa did his thing.

That changed the year my father enlisted me to help make my mother's Christmas wish come true.

Right after Thanksgiving Mom mentioned how nice it would be to have a Christmas manger in our front window that was visible from the sidewalk without being mistaken for a matchbox. The tiny cardboard model, a treasure from her childhood, obviously was no longer suitable. Dad responded with a joke about its size, but I knew he took her request straight to his heart.

Not long after that, Dad arrived home from picket-line duty one day with four old orange crates. I followed him down the cellar steps and back to his workshop.

"What are *they* for?"

"A Christmas manger scene for the front window. Didn't you hear Mom say the other night that she wanted one?"

"I heard her, but how can you make anything decent out of a bunch of scrap orange crates?"

Dad chuckled and said, "Scrap, huh? You'll see."

Dad was a fine craftsman and an obsessive perfectionist. Having Dad sign my homework was proof of that, because he didn't let me get away with anything except my best. I learned never to try to hand my schoolwork to Dad with blatant eraser marks or cross outs. When a school project didn't pass his inspection, I redid it—sometimes more than once—until my work was something he could be proud of, even if it didn't make any difference to me. Because I knew of the strict demands he made on himself, I wondered how he could turn that pile of scrap wood into something that Mom would like.

After that, each night I gulped down my supper and finished my homework (taking extra care not to leave eraser marks or to cross out anything). Once I knew it was the best I could do, I raced down the cellar steps to my father's workshop.

He worked on the crèche only about an hour each night. "There's plenty of time to finish it before Christmas," he said several times.

I was fascinated as I watched Dad measure, sketch, and study my mom's little cardboard version. He scrutinized models pictured in the Sears, Roebuck catalog. I kept waiting for him to start cutting, but he'd say, "Not yet." He wanted to make certain he knew exactly what he was doing and what he wanted to accomplish before he cut a single piece of wood.

For a couple of weeks, it still looked like nothing but scrap lumber to me. But once he began to work, those old orange crates no longer resembled scrap.

During these nightly workshop sessions, Dad taught me how to use a miter box and a carpenter's square. From him I learned the difference between a wood screw and a machine screw and how to use a vice and C-clamps. I carefully followed his instructions no matter what job he gave me to do. I was determined to make him proud of my efforts.

I learned a little about woodworking back then, but that wasn't the most important thing. I learned about my dad as I watched him pour his heart and soul into a pile of old orange crates.

After he assembled all the pieces, with minor assistance from me, the crèche stood twenty-four inches tall at the peak of its pitched roof, with a solid back wall into which Daddy cut a hole and placed a single white light. Securing it high at the top of the back wall kept the bulb out of plain sight from the front and provided a warmly illuminated interior. A low barnyard-style fence filled in the sides at the base and went around to the front, which allowed an unobstructed view of the inside.

After that, Dad and I painted it dark brown except for one small patch on the inside of the roof where I could still see some of the orange crate advertising. But to see that spot, I had to stick my head all the way inside and look up.

Daddy pointed to that spot and said, "Whenever you doubt the possibility of making something out of nothing, remember that patch of wood and think about what we had when we started."

On the Saturday before Christmas, when it was time to put up our decorations, Daddy brought Mom down to the basement and unveiled our recycled orange crate surprise. To this day I can't forget the look of delight on Mom's face when she saw it. "Oh, it's such a beautiful, beautiful manger crèche."

Mom's old figurines, chipped from years of wear, just wouldn't do for the new masterpiece. Besides being chipped, they were too small for our expanded version.

Despite the tightness of money, Mom and I put on our coats and hats and rode the trolley to the local Woolworth's store. She bought new figurines of Mary, Joseph, baby Jesus, one donkey, and a mother sheep with two lambs. It cost her three dollars. That was quite a sum of cash for such tough times. (As the years went by and Dad was back at work, they added the shepherds, wise men, and other nonessential characters and animals, one or two each year.)

By the time Mom and I arrived home, Dad had already set up our new manger scene in the center of the picture window that looked out from our enclosed front porch. Strewn about on the sill was sweet-smelling straw given to him by a friend who owned a farm. I thought, *I've never smelled anything so nice.*

After it grew dark, all three of us stood in front of the house to stare at the picture window and be the first to enjoy the opening night of our new Christmas display. Mary and Joseph knelt close to baby Jesus, who looked quite serene as the warm golden glow of light fell softly upon their faces.

"I've never seen anything so beautiful," Mom said several times.

I felt happy and contented because the manger was a gift from Dad's heart and from mine.

That was the best Christmas I can remember. That part is so vivid, but I can't remember what surprises Santa brought that year. The time I spent with Dad making Mom's manger scene was the *real* Christmas gift.

Mom and Dad have now been in heaven for many years. Putting up the crèche every year for Christmas is a gift I give to myself. The meaning and memories attached to it make Christmas complete even if I never open another present.

I have the best gift; I don't need anything else.

28. The Forgotten Gift

Viola Shimp with Cindy Thomson

ONE KIND OF SHOPPING TRIP AT CHRISTMASTIME THAT I have always looked forward to is to buy a gift for someone who will never know my identity. For me, that's the kind of gift that makes Christmas meaningful.

Each year our church puts up a Christmas tree decorated with paper ornaments. This is similar to what some call the Angel Tree.

Each ornament is inscribed with something a needy child in our community wants for Christmas, such as clothes, a game, or books. A local elementary school sends the requests to us. Our pastor invites us to choose an ornament or two and buy whatever the child wants.

After we buy the gift, we wrap it and designate which ornament we selected. A few weeks before Christmas, a committee sorts the gifts and coordinates delivery to the families. In addition, our church provides food for the families.

I choose ornaments designated for baby gifts. It's a blessing to me to know that a little child will have at least one adorable, warm outfit at Christmastime and a little toy to go with it.

As I was shopping one day for something to accompany the outfit I had picked out, I struck up a conversation with a fellow shopper in the toy department. I hadn't met the woman before, but we were both looking through the baby toys trying to choose something special.

"Who are you shopping for?" she asked.

I explained about our church's project. She appeared to be interested, so I went on to tell her about the special challenge our church undertook each year. "This year, we have far more gifts than usual to buy," I explained, remembering the vast number of ornaments that covered the tree.

She nodded to show she understood.

"So many people are out of work in our community and unable to buy gifts for their children. The pastor said there are more than two hundred and fifty gifts requested."

The number seemed to shock her, but she said, "That's wonderful that you are helping." She smiled and asked, "What are you looking for?"

"I already have part of the gift, but I like to include a toy. What's Christmas without toys?"

"Here's a lovely little noisemaker," she said, holding the soft toy out to me. "It's only five dollars."

"I think that will do fine. Thanks for helping me."

She went on her way and I continued to look around. A few minutes later the woman came down the store aisle toward me with her hand outstretched. "I think it's so wonderful what your church is doing for the unemployed in our community. I want to help." She handed me a ten-dollar bill.

I thanked her and hugged her.

When I got home, I called Laura, the woman in charge of the ornament project at church.

"The school just came by and picked up all the leftover ornaments," she said. "I started to gather the wrapped gifts from
under the tree to prepare to sort them, and I discovered one
ornament that had fallen off the tree. It had been hidden under
the presents."

"How awful," I said.

"I've been trying to decide what to do. It's too late to ask the
congregation to help and school is closed for the holidays." She
had been pondering what to do when I called. "The church helpers are about ready to deliver the presents."

I told her about the woman donating ten dollars. "Will that
help?"

"Yes! Yes! I can buy that gift," she said. "God has provided."

I would have loved to have been able to purchase more gifts
that Christmas, but I'm on a limited income. I have taught Sunday school for many years, and I tell my little charges who are
excited about the gifts and the wonderful happenings Christmas
brings that it isn't the gifts that are most important at Christmas.
It's the spirit of love in which those gifts are given that reflects
God's love for His people and His gift of Jesus.

That shopping trip and the encounter with the woman whose
name I will never know reminded me of another truth. God
showed me that day that He provides for even those whom we
have forgotten.

When needs are ignored or neglected by others, even uninten-
tionally, God still knows about them. He knew that a little
child's wish had been lost behind the wrapped gifts under the
church's Christmas tree.

Sometimes our best efforts of generosity and giving fall short.

God makes up the rest even when we don't know there is more to do.

The realization of what had happened on my favorite shopping trip that year, and the fact that God used me in His plan to provide for that gift, continues to warm my heart to this day.

29. His Special Gift

Susan Titus Osborn

AWAKENING TO THE BRIGHT CALIFORNIA SUN STREAMING in my bedroom window, I realized it was my first Christmas morning as a single parent. I had been separated for less than two months from my husband of twenty-two years.

I dreaded the approaching Christmas season and the emotions aroused by past remembrances. I lay in bed and thought back to the morning my husband, looking tired and tense, walked into the kitchen, sat down at the breakfast table, and said, "I care about you, but I don't love you enough to live with you anymore."

When I heard those words, my world crumbled. I had sensed that things weren't right between us, but it hadn't occurred to me that he wanted out of our marriage. We had been going to a Christian counselor for six months, but that apparently didn't make any difference. As far as my husband was concerned, the marriage was dead.

And when he spoke those words, part of me died with the marriage, because so much of my life revolved around my husband.

The uncertainty of my future scared me. I didn't know if I would be able to support myself and my two sons as a freelance writer. I hadn't yet earned a college degree and I didn't know what else I could do to earn a living. My husband felt a woman's place was in the home, so I hadn't worked full-time in nineteen years.

I wasn't sure if I would receive any spousal support or if my husband would help the boys with their college expenses. Plus, I had college expenses of my own to pay because I was studying part-time to earn my BA in religious studies. I was trying to help my son Richard, who attended the University of California at Santa Barbara. My other son, Mike, was a senior in high school.

I worked at a local Christian university part-time, but that was only for a few hours a week and it didn't pay the bills.

Yet in spite of our tight finances, God had provided extra money in the form of a book royalty check so I could buy my sons needed items as well as some fun ones for Christmas.

Richard came home from college for the holidays, and Mike was on his Christmas break. The past few days we had enjoyed some quality time together before our busy schedules resumed.

I got out of bed, threw on my robe, and rushed downstairs to cook our traditional Christmas breakfast of bacon, eggs, and my homemade coffee cake. After we asked the Lord to bless the food, we sat around the breakfast table making small talk.

"The girls in the apartment next to us played a funny trick on us a couple of months ago," Richard said. "They had borrowed our vacuum cleaner, and when they returned it one of them sneaked over to our phone and without our realizing it changed the message on our answering machine to something silly."

We all laughed. Mike told about a funny incident that had happened at his holiday job. We laughed again. It felt so good to have laughter at the table once again. Meals had been tense the last few months my husband had lived with us.

After we finished eating, I cleared the table and thought about how fortunate I was to have two teenagers who shared the little events in their lives with me. We moved into the family room, sat around the Christmas tree, and started opening our presents.

"You know, Mom, even though there's less under the tree this year, somehow it seems to mean more," Richard said. "Being home for my vacation with you and Mike matters a lot, too. Funny, I just took this for granted before."

"I'll be honest, guys. I've been a little apprehensive about the holidays. There have been so many changes in our lives the past two months—" I tried to put my emotions into coherent thoughts. "I know the divorce has been as hard for both of you as it has for me."

"I was afraid somehow that we wouldn't be a family anymore," Mike said. "I mean that we wouldn't feel like a family or something, but that hasn't happened."

"We're still a family," Richard said emphatically. "The only difference is we're now a family of three instead of four."

"Being together is what matters," I added. "I enjoyed having both of you here for the midnight service at church last night."

With Richard 150 miles away at college, we didn't often get a chance to worship together.

After most of the packages were opened, Mike handed me a white envelope as my last present—his Christmas gift to me. I knew he hadn't worked many hours since summer, so his finances were tighter than mine. Water polo season had recently ended, and I wanted him to keep up his studies. He worked only a handful of hours each weekend as a community service leader at our city's recreational center. His job was to sign people up for the swimming pool, gym, and racquetball courts.

I looked up, and Mike's gaze met mine. "Well, open it," he said.

I slit the envelope open. Inside was a handwritten gift certificate that read: "Good for one oil change and a tire rotation."

Tears filled my eyes as I hugged my younger son. Mike's gift would save me money, and I desperately needed my oil changed and my tires rotated. However, it meant far more than helping my meager budget.

Mike had given me the greatest gift he had to offer—his time. He had given himself. Between his studies and his part-time job, he had little free time, and he'd used it to help take care of me.

At a time when I felt alone, adrift, and uncertain, his gift reminded me that I was loved and supported. I was also reminded that God wouldn't ever stop loving me or move out of my life—a message I've never forgotten.

30. The Most Beautiful-Ugly Christmas Ornament

Kelly J. Stigliana

My company assigned me to Gretis Morris's case. I was to prepare her meals, do light housekeeping, and keep her company. She lived in what is commonly called a mother-in-law suite, which was attached to her daughter's house in Columbus, Ohio. Gretis's daughter and son-in-law took good care of her, but because they both taught full-time, they needed someone to come in one day each week to help.

Mrs. Morris accepted me as family almost immediately. A native of West Virginia, she often spoke of her home there and the friends she had made throughout her seventy-eight years of life.

Through her stories, I felt the warmth and friendship of her small Appalachian community through the lean years and the joy of prosperity in the occasional income. The camaraderie in the "holler" village she described rivaled that of Walnut Grove in the *Little House on the Prairie* TV series.

When the company through which I worked demanded more of my time, I had to quit. My contract stated that I couldn't work independently for any of their clients and receive payment. I spoke with Mrs. Morris and decided I wanted to continue to help her without charging. I would come when she called to say she needed me.

My own grandmother had died eleven years earlier, and Mrs.

Morris became my new gramma. My children occasionally accompanied me to her house and she loved them as much as if they were her grandchildren. My children's grandparents lived several hours away, so her kindness filled that emptiness in their lives.

We had delightful times together. I repotted her houseplants, cleaned her house, rearranged her pantry, changed her bedding, plucked her chin hairs, and listened (and relistened) to her stories of a hard life in the hills of Appalachia. Without my being aware, through her quiet lessons I learned about living, marriage, and parenting style.

Each Christmas we exchanged gifts. She bought me the same gift she bought her daughter: a nightshirt, floral slip-on sneakers, and potholders. I adored each one and the gifts made me feel that I was part of the family.

One Christmas, Mrs. Morris sent a wrapped gift with me. At home I opened my package and found, alongside the gift, a little ball of white tissue paper containing an old, faded pink glass tree ornament. It was not only quite ugly, but it also was scratched and slightly resembled a small pinecone. I thought, *Surely this is a mistake.*

When I spoke with her the next time I asked her if she knew she had put an ornament inside the box.

"Oh yes. I thought you'd like to have it."

I thanked her and put it away and said to myself, *Maybe I'll use it next Christmas.*

Another year passed. One chilly winter week Mrs. Morris didn't call. She sometimes missed a week, but when I received no call after a second week I became concerned. I phoned her daughter and she said that Gretis was in the hospital "and they don't expect her to live."

I visited her in the hospital and she smiled weakly at me. With half-awake eyes she thanked me for coming.

It was December and I told her that I thought the best way to spend Christmas was with the Christ Child himself. She smiled and nodded.

Three days later, on December 15, Gretis Morris, my second gramma, died. They took her to her hometown of Clendenin, West Virginia, to be buried.

After her death, I didn't feel like decorating our house for Christmas, but I pushed myself to do so. When I finally got to my tree ornaments I saw that ugly old pink pinecone. As I held it in my hand and stared at it, I thought of the many Christmases it had seen in the mountains of West Virginia, the happy Christmases and probably a few stressful Christmases.

As I stared, I realized what a special gift Gretis had given me. I saw it as the most beautiful ornament I'd ever laid eyes on and carefully placed it at the top of our tree, close to the trunk so it wouldn't fall.

It became my most treasured ornament. Each year I carefully unwrap it and fondly remember Mrs. Morris as I place it on the tree. That old pink ornament glistens in the soft glow of the twinkling lights. It shines down on our family each year as we celebrate the birth of Jesus together.

Over the years we have moved around, and our celebrations have gotten smaller as the children moved away. Each year I look at that pink ornament tucked up high on the tree and remember the year I received it. The kids were little then and, like many families, we struggled financially. That dear old ornament has seen our happy Christmases and our stressful Christmases.

Season after season I reflect on the life lessons Mrs. Morris passed on to me. I know that with God's help it is possible to remain strong and loving through all of life's trials.

Each Christmas I pray that, in the year to come, I will touch at least one life the way Mrs. Morris touched mine. Because that's what Christmas and this life really mean: the lives we touch, the people we love, and the precious moments we spend together.

31. The Scrinch

Ruth Kaufman

WHEN IT COMES TO THE HOLIDAYS, I'VE BEEN A SCRINCH—a made-up word that's a combination of *Scrooge* and *Grinch*. My great-uncle's birthday was December 25, so our family gatherings were more about his birthday and everyone having the day off from work than they were about anything religious or spiritual.

I've since realized that there is too much preparation, too much money spent, too many hours of cleaning up, and too few minutes of eating and unwrapping gifts.

Despite all the hurry and push, I auditioned for Winter WonderFest (WWF), a 170,000-square-foot indoor holiday amusement park attended by thousands each day at Festival Hall in Navy Pier, Chicago's most popular tourist attraction.

Friends asked me why I'd want to be a costumed character who spent more than 160 hours immersed in Christmas cheer, surrounded by thousands of ornaments, hundreds of decorated Christmas trees, and inundated by holiday music and the ever-present aromas of funnel cakes, caramel corn, and cinnamon-coated nuts.

I did it because WWF is a paying improv gig—a job hard to find in Chicago's thriving improv community. I also do it because any kind of paid acting work is particularly hard to find in December.

I had no expectations at the audition. I did a couple of short group exercises, including a slow-motion race and a scene as the character I was auditioning for, Major Nougat of the Candy Corps.

I wanted the opportunity to work with talented people. When I got the call that I'd been cast, I looked forward to the rehearsal process when we'd develop our characters and community. My costume was a long underskirt with candy cane stripes and a red overskirt with a bustle and many petticoats. I wore a green satin breastplate with candy medals, and candy on my epaulettes. Besides that I wore a red wig and cute red hat with gold braid.

My partner, Colonel Caramel, and the ten other Winter WonderFriends developed so many interesting aspects of our characters and fun things to do that I could hardly wait for our grand opening to try them out.

We began with a short opening ceremony. Attendees gathered in the hallway with Mayor Burl Evergreen and his secretary, Miss Tannenbaum, and they led a countdown to exactly 10:00 A.M. As choral music sounded, a huge garage door lifted and revealed the rest of our members.

While traveling the vast hall (my pedometer tallied more than five miles per shift) we entertained and engaged as many patrons as possible. They ranged from babies (the youngest I met was born on Christmas Eve) to school groups, families, couples, and seniors.

Each day we played new games and learned different ways to make people laugh. Besides posing for hundreds of pictures and signing autographs, our activities included holding imaginary tea parties and acting out stories made up on the spot. Creating tales and playing with the other actors who had become friends was delightful, and it challenged our creativity.

The Colonel and I encouraged groups of kids to march with us and create new, silly ways to march. We collected high fives and patrolled long lines at the huge Ferris wheel and other rides, encouraging people to salute and shout, "This is for the Candy Corps!" I enjoyed having such an outlandishly loud and physically active role.

When certain songs played, all Winter WonderFriends stopped whatever they were doing and raced to the entrance to hold a dance party. Having patrons join us or simply smile and laugh at our antics made those moments memorable for me.

We served as attorneys in Bah Humbug Court to defend those ticketed by Winter WonderForce officers Eddie and Doug for infractions such as insufficient holiday attire, beleaguered picture taking, or Scrooge-like behavior.

Several times the Colonel and I had the honor of escorting Santa around the Fest. Of course kids liked to sit on Santa's lap, but I hadn't grasped the wonder and sheer admiration kids had for him. Those children who engaged Santa in a Nerf snowball fight or went down huge inflatable slides with him roared with joy.

A popular game with patrons of all ages was Silent Night at the Museum, created by the rag dolls, Holly and Berry. Whoever was named "it" yelled, "Go!" Players raced around until the command "Freeze!"

Everyone instantly became a statue in a museum. "It" tried to make each player laugh and accumulated helpers as each statue succumbed to giggles. The last one standing would be "it" for the next round. Not only did huge crowds gather to watch, but the kids' commitment to that game astonished me. One girl had frozen with her tongue out and her arms splayed. She didn't budge no matter how hard trained actors tried to break her concentration and make her laugh. Of course she became the next "it."

One of my favorite things was to infiltrate family photos. Whenever we saw people posing, Colonel Caramel and I ran as fast as we could to get into the picture. Watching the photographer's expression change from intent concentration, to surprise, to joy when we appeared in the viewfinder didn't get tiresome. The photographer nearly always burst out laughing and saying, "Yes, yes," or, "Wait," while refocusing to include us in the shot.

The subjects of the photos welcomed us and usually hugged us, which warmed me like a swig of hot chocolate. One photographer was so tickled by our infiltration she couldn't stop laughing. Repeatedly she said, "I'm filled with joy."

Those words, of course, filled me with joy—all because I'd been enlisted to bring enjoyment and laughter to so many people.

On occasion I'd twirl around in time to the music because it was fun to make my full skirts and petticoats whirl. One time I started spinning near a group of teenagers. They followed me. The freedom to whirl and whoop, to be silly and loud together, created a memorable moment.

I enjoyed watching expressions of awe on visitors' faces. Most kids' faces lit up with excitement when they saw us. They usually ran over to talk, play, or snap a picture. Many gave me a hug.

A few kids were frightened or shy and hid behind their parents. So we developed games to draw them out. If we didn't get them to take a picture with us, usually we got at least a high five. Making those kids smile was especially rewarding.

So why did I, a professed Scrinch, work at Winter Wonder-

Fest? At first, I had done it for the paycheck, but the reward I took away was much bigger. Every time I made someone laugh or saw a kid's eyes widen with wonder or a child gave me a hug or sat on my lap, my Scrinch's heart grew. I felt something I'd never experienced before and won't lose again: the holiday spirit.

32. The SPCA Christmas

Nancy Haag

WE'D SPENT SEVERAL CHRISTMASES ALONE; THIS ONE WOULD be no exception. We couldn't afford to fly to be with our family. Because of the distance we had too little time to drive. Scotty, my husband, and I decided to look for people who might consider spending Christmas in our home. We'd done that in another state, and it had been special each time.

We invited a man from our square dancing class. Divorced and alone, he also battled alcohol addiction. After that, we invited a young couple at church, who'd recently relocated to the Southwest from Alaska.

Scotty came home and said that a colleague, his wife, and two children would have to spend their holiday separated from their extended family. Our neighbors, a retired, childless couple, also had nowhere to go.

We invited a couple with two small boys who had decided not to celebrate Christmas because of finances. I'd been introduced to a recent widow, who planned to eat alone in a Chinese restaurant.

Two days before Christmas, Scotty and I counted and the total was thirty, of whom eleven were children. We emptied a back bedroom and set it up for the kids. I called each mother to say, "Bring their new toys, because we have plenty of space."

Scotty and I decorated the tree with Life Savers, animal crackers, candy canes, and lollipops in the colors of Christmas. I also invited the women to bring a favorite dish, and several promised food that had been part of their own back-home tradition. This was shaping up to be even more than the Merry Christmas Scotty and I had wanted.

Scotty and I had been hauling wood for the fireplace, decorating the doors, and setting out luminarias when Lisa, our teenager, came home after visiting with friends. After she dropped her coat and took off her boots, she saw the plates, boxes, and bags. "Mom! Who is coming this time? *Please* not another SPCA Christmas!"

I wouldn't have put it that way. Lisa labeled it after the SPCA—the Society for the Prevention of Cruelty to Animals, which adopts lost and stray animals—because she immediately thought of it as our gathering in lost and unwanted strangers as we had done before.

"Yes, we've invited a few new friends and several strangers," I said. "No one should be alone and not celebrating." Although I didn't say it, with our frequent relocations Christmas had often been difficult for me. Creating a sense of community made it infinitely more bearable.

Determined to ignore my daughter's comments, I reminded her that the Bible says: "Don't forget to show hospitality to strangers, for some who have done this have entertained angels without realizing it" (Hebrews 13:2).

With her back to me, she shrugged.

"Okay, then, how about 1 Peter 4:9?" I picked up my Bible and read: " 'Cheerfully share your home with those who need a meal or a place to stay.' "

"So?"

"So," I said, "how about helping me round up chairs, and we'll need two more tables." Just as I looked around, her bedroom door slammed.

Scotty offered to make phone calls and to borrow chairs and a table from neighbors. At our house, we sometimes dragged picnic benches from the backyard and pulled out our ancient card table. I didn't mind what they looked like because my festive tablecloths would pull everything together, along with candles, paper Christmas plates, and matching napkins. In the meantime, I pretended not to hear my daughter's, "I can't believe it!"

The following day, our guests began arriving early with favorite foods and the children carried their new toys. Within minutes, the cleared bedroom became the setting for LEGO towers, dolls, buggies, games, and books. Most of our guests didn't know anyone in the house but us, but it didn't take long for them to make new friends. Several exchanged telephone numbers for future use.

Despite her attitude the day before, Lisa helped by entertaining the younger children and, later, assisted with the after-midnight cleanup. She didn't say much about the day and she didn't complain, so I didn't think any more about it.

Several years ago, after Lisa married, she invited Scotty and me to her home for Christmas.

Scotty and I traveled across three states to get there, so I was tired. Nevertheless, I was still eager to help set up what I knew would be a beautiful table. Not only that, but I had so much to share with and to hear from her also.

In the middle of our sharing and peeling yams, I realized Lisa had set her table for fifteen people. "We're only six," I said as my daughter dropped down in front of her buffet to find her prettiest napkins and a box of Christmas candles. "So, who else—?"

Over her shoulder Lisa called back, "I've invited a couple of friends."

I'd hoped for a quiet, family dinner, but we would be sharing it with her friends—yes, her friends, but strangers to me.

"I just hope they get along," she said, deciding on dessert plates and wineglasses.

"You hope *who* gets along? If they're all friends—"

"Those people who don't know anyone but me," she said.

"They don't know—? But they're all coming for dinner and—?" I could hardly believe what she said. Lisa prided herself on keeping her dinners simple. "So the guests will be—?"

"A woman from down the street," Lisa said without looking directly at me. "She moved here from New York after her divorce, and she's lonely."

"That's nice," I said. "And—?"

"And a couple with their first baby, because her mother doesn't want to spend Christmas with them and Sarah doesn't get along all that well with her parents." Lisa rearranged a lavish bouquet of red flowers. "Oh yes, and there's a girl from the bank, and also a couple with two little girls who just moved here from California. He doesn't have work yet. And I've asked a woman whose husband has been diagnosed with Alzheimer's. Christmas is really hard for her." My daughter picked up a divided silver dish for the candies and nuts. "So—"

"So," I said, "we're going to have—?" I couldn't say the word. I stared at her and grinned.

"Yes, Mom. I'm having an SPCA Christmas." She tipped her head. "Okay?"

"Okay," I said as I turned back toward the kitchen to count the glasses and cups and to keep my laughter to myself. She wouldn't admit it, but my daughter had understood about opening up our home—even to near strangers. Now she filled her arms with the baskets that would hold her dozens of cookies and loaves of bread.

"Maybe you would choose the music," she said, "while I set up the coffee."

"I'll be glad to do that." I turned and gazed intently at my child. "And, honey—"

Her face hinted of a smile.

"Merry Christmas," I said.

"Merry Christmas, Mom."

33. The Pause That Refreshes

Susan Green

AS A LITTLE GIRL I SAW BILLBOARDS AND MAGAZINE ADVER-
tisements of a cherry-cheeked Santa Claus, eyes twinkling and
head back, enjoying Coca-Cola. The words were "The pause
that refreshes."

As I've pondered that childhood experience, it makes me realize that through our days of busyness leading up to Christmas
and the New Year we can choose to take "a pause that refreshes."
Amid our finishing work projects before leaving for the Christmas
holiday, during our times of last-minute shopping, cooking, and
decorating, we can plan simple pauses to refresh our souls. We
can enjoy God's company and allow His agenda to overrule ours.

In our house, we tend to stuff the stocking of our days full to
overflowing, not wanting to miss anything and wanting everything about the season to be extraspecial. Through the years,
there were times of overplanning, overbuying, overdecorating,
overbaking, and overspending. And I admit that often I was glad
when the season was over and said, "I'm anything but refreshed."

Forgetting past seasons of overdoing, I set aside a day to accomplish many things. I filled my day with an ambitious list, starting with preparing for the Advent season through reading and
prayer, followed closely by cleaning parts of the house, putting

up Christmas decorations, baking cookies, and then I felt sure I would still have time to meet a friend for Christmas tea and maybe pick up a few things at the mall.

Reading and prayer were at the top of my list that morning, but as I snuggled down with my coffee I couldn't keep my attention centered on what I had just read. My mind had already engaged in what I should/would/could do throughout the day. It was increasingly difficult for me to stay still, relax, and enjoy time with God.

I struggled and tension filled my body. As if the question came out of nowhere, I asked myself, *What do I really want?*

I want to enjoy this day, I answered myself. *I want to spend it with God.*

As I heard my own thought, I asked God to help me set aside my to-do list and give me what I most wanted and needed. I asked Him to plan my day.

I sat quietly and slowed down. Rather than speed-reading to accomplish as much as I could in one sitting, I read a few verses from the Bible, played and listened to Christmas carols as I sat quietly.

After a relaxed time of silence, I opened a box. As I put up the nativity scene I thought about Mary and Joseph. What a beginning they had to their new life together. How different married life must have been from what they had imagined. That young woman, whom future generations would call blessed, started her life as a new wife and mother under a cloud of suspicion. Joseph showed us what love looks like by his protecting, trusting, hoping, persevering—a living picture to show that true love never fails.

I pondered the Christmas story as I went through the day's activities. I decided not to hurry and I wasn't anxious. I went from one thing to the next, resting when I got tired and took time for a nap. To my surprise, I accomplished a great deal and finished most of the things on my list, but not all.

And it didn't matter. I ended the day with a full, restful, and thankful heart—that's what I truly wanted. Whether we have a day or a few hours to get things done, it's amazing what taking small breaks in the midst of busyness can do to unhurry us.

Those of us who are list makers and list checkers can feel a sense of accomplishment and relief as we finish one project and move on to the next. It's a good feeling to get things done. But what if we also scheduled pauses into our project lists?

That's what I learned when I asked myself what I truly wanted. It was all right (even refreshing) to put up my feet for a few minutes in the middle of my cleaning.

If you can't take an hour for your devotions, what about reading the Christmas story in pieces and taking that part of the story with you into your vacuuming or cookie baking? While doing for everyone else, fix yourself a warm drink. Sit down to enjoy the lights on your own tree for a few minutes before you move to the next thing on your list. A five-minute break now and then can recharge your energy and help you enjoy more of your holidays.

It's difficult not to feel we're wasting time when there is so much to do. I've learned, however, that pacing ourselves isn't wasting time. It's conserving our energy. It may also relax us and make the rest of the events of the day go smoother.

We can speed through our daily details like race-car drivers with Christmas scenery rushing past us, or we can pace ourselves and enjoy the details of our day.

Accept God's invitation throughout the days of this special season. Relax in the occasion and allow the spirit of Christmas to invade and possess your heart. Take a pause that refreshes. Slow your pace and you may become kinder to everyone, especially to yourself. You'll spend and end your days with a full heart.

And, next year, you might remember this year's holiday scenery.

34. Confession of the Christmas Damper

Brenda Poinsett

"DON'T EXPECT MUCH," MY HUSBAND, BOB, SAID THE YEAR he had been out of work for six months. Although he had started to work in November, he hadn't been on the job long enough for us to get caught up with the accumulated bills. We didn't want to add to our debt, so we decided to spend very little for Christmas.

For ten dollars we bought a marked-down Christmas tree with a crooked trunk. While our sons decorated it, they began talking about Christmas morning, when they would open gifts. I decided that I'd better stop that kind of talk. "Now, boys, don't expect much for Christmas this year." I explained (again) the reason.

"Sure, Mom," they said.

TV commercials especially designed to make children want expensive toys captured our sons' attention. They dreamed aloud about what they would get. When they did that and I heard them, I interrupted with, "Remember, boys, don't expect much this Christmas."

As Ben and his friend Bruce drove their trucks over the carpet, they chattered about the toys they wanted. When Bruce left, I said, "Now, Ben, don't expect much for Christmas."

I had said the *don't expect much* words so many times that I felt like a new Christmas character was developing—a character to take her place right along with Ebenezer Scrooge and the

Grinch. She was Christmas Damper. The minute she heard boys and girls expressing their Christmas wishes, she threw water on them. Her goal was to put out the fires of Christmas expectation.

Jim, almost a teenager, began to spend a lot of time in his room with the door closed. Joel, two years younger, was listless. Saying he didn't have anything to do, he leaned on my desk while I tried to work. Ben acted babyish and wanted to sit on my lap like he did when he was younger.

Christmas gloom settled over our house.

If anyone had told me in November that this would happen, I would have said, "Not at my house." I had been certain that having little money to spend wouldn't seriously affect the quality of our celebration because I try hard to emphasize the meaning of the season. This year, though, the Advent candles no longer held an attractive glow. Our daily December devotions, an activity the boys normally welcomed, no longer seemed of interest.

When our pastor preached a sermon blaming the loss of meaning on the busyness of Christmas, I thought, *Bah! Humbug!* I hadn't bought one ribbon, gift tag, or sheet of wrapping paper. We weren't caught up in the busy activity of buying gifts for the holidays.

During those pre-Christmas days, Carileen, a real estate agent for whom I sometimes worked, called: "I've decided to have an open house. Would you bake the cookies, prepare the punch, and serve them?"

I welcomed the job. *Perhaps baking thirty dozen cookies and preparing punch will get my thoughts off our gloomy Christmas.* It did while I shopped for the ingredients, but as I rolled the dough for the sugar cookies I thought of my mother, five hundred miles away. Right then, she was probably also baking. During the holidays, people came and went at Mother's house and she offered pie and coffee to each one. Warmth permeated her home.

How did Mother achieve that holiday warmth? How did she develop an atmosphere where people felt they could stop by? Did it take years of living in a community for people to feel that comfortable? Did it happen only when relatives lived near?

Our family had no relatives in our area, and we hadn't lived in our community long. Thinking about the warmth in my mother's house made the Christmas gloom hang even heavier.

The morning of Carileen's open house, I wrote in my journal: "There's something wrong with this Christmas. Sadness prevails. My family isn't excited or happy about the season. I don't want it to be this way. I want something more."

"Lord Jesus," I prayed, "I've tried to honor you at Christmas. Help me to identify our problem and to see how to correct it."

I loaded the cookies, the serving trays, the punch, and the punch bowl and went to Carileen's. I kept the punch bowl filled and cookies on the trays while her clients came and went. Hearing their laughter and talk, I felt a warmth—a warmth similar to what permeated my mother's house. At Mother's, they came and went because they knew her. At Carileen's, people came and went because they were invited. If I wanted to create warmth at my own home, perhaps I needed to invite people.

When I got home, I said to Bob and the boys, "I have an idea. I know this sounds crazy, but let's have an open house."

"No one will come," Bob said. "Everyone we know will be spending Christmas with their families."

"Perhaps we could ask them to stop by Christmas Eve afternoon for a few minutes on the way to wherever they are going," I said.

"But you've been reminding us all month how little money we have. How can we afford an open house?" Jim asked.

"People won't eat much if they're on their way to some other place. Besides, I learned this week that a five-pound sack of flour makes a lot of cookies. We could serve cookies and punch."

"What about postage for the invitations?" Bob asked.

"Let's hand deliver them. We could give them out at church, and you kids can take them to school. You can invite whomever you want."

When I said that, their eyes lit up. "Let's do it," they said.

We had fun handing out invitations to people we knew well, to people we wanted to know better, to strangers, and to people in situations like our own.

With just a few days left before Christmas, Joel, Ben, and I baked cookies and cleaned house. The weather was unseasonably warm, so we opened the windows. We polished the furniture and shook the rugs. Anyone driving by our country home would have thought we were doing our spring housecleaning.

About thirty minutes before it was time for the open house to begin, we had everything ready. The boys kept opening the front door to look down the road to see if anyone was coming. After several looks, they sat down. Joel said, "Can you believe we finally have everything ready?"

I used that moment to remind them that Jesus came into the world when God had everything ready: "God planned and made special arrangements for Jesus' birth. God picked out a name, chose a birthplace, and prepared the people by promising them from time to time that Jesus would come. Now that we understand what it takes to get ready for something important, let's thank God for preparing the world for Jesus' coming."

We stopped and prayed. Just as we finished, the doorbell rang. The first guest had arrived. During the afternoon thirty-seven people came—just the right number. Their coming and going stretched out over the afternoon, so there was time for leisurely conversation.

Although most were on their way to other places, they seemed to enjoy the relaxed atmosphere of our home. While they were there, the gloom departed and warmth arrived. It lingered long after the last guest departed.

From the time we started planning our open house, the boys no longer talked about what they were going to *get* for Christmas. Gifts no longer mattered. In a year when we didn't have much, we learned that celebration of the real purpose of Christmas is what matters.

35. Twenty Dollars

Terry Nelson

ABOUT THE AGE OF SEVEN, WITH CHRISTMAS A DAY OR TWO away, I yearned to open the large, colorful, beautifully wrapped packages with my name on them.

Even when I was young, I was allowed to stay up late. My dad or mom would remind me to turn off the television and the lights before going to bed. They trusted me and didn't worry. There was no alcohol for me to get into, no cigarettes to smoke, nothing to get me into any trouble.

Nothing, that is, except when a seven-year-old boy is left alone with a stack of Christmas presents with his name on them.

As part of our family tradition, one week before Christmas my parents placed the gifts under the Christmas tree, which had already been up for a week or two. Without anything underneath its wide-spreading low branches the tree looked bare. To me it was that way even with glittering tinsel, brightly decorated ornaments, lights burning red, white, blue, green, and orange. But once my parents put presents under the Christmas tree, the room took on a warm glow. Even the tree looked fuller, richer, more beautiful, giving depth and dimension. The presents were piled up and the low tree branches seemed almost to reach out to hug those pretty packages.

That Christmas, I sat on the floor watching television. Mom

and Dad were asleep. All was quiet. What could I do during commercials of *The Steve Allen Show*?

I checked the tags on the wrapped gifts to see which were mine. I noted the large packages first and moved down to the small boxes, which I hoped were for someone else.

I didn't want little packages, because there couldn't be any good toys in small boxes. I carefully moved the packages, always putting them back exactly as I found them, making sure not to disturb anything. I couldn't see through the wrapping paper and I couldn't peel away Scotch Tape without drawing attention to my tampering. Parents seem to know if kids make even the slightest rip.

After checking all the name tags, I spotted an envelope with my name on the front. When I turned it over, my eyebrows arched in surprise. It hadn't been sealed. *Probably a dumb old card*, I thought. But I opened it anyway, and before I could read it I noticed a twenty-dollar bill.

Twenty dollars! I would be rich. It was unheard of for a kid in our neighborhood in the 1950s to get such a large amount of money.

Carefully I put the card back into the envelope and placed it where I had found it. I thought of spending the money. I could buy a lot of football and baseball cards with that kind of money. I dreamed of comic books and neat toys that didn't come from Santa's bag.

Christmas Eve came, and after dinner my dad sat on the sofa, my mother in a large overstuffed, comfortable chair. I was to distribute the presents, and after passing a few out, I came to the card.

I was quite nonchalant. I decided to act surprised and to be very thankful. Playing cops and robbers had made me good at pretending. "Here is a card for me," I said. "I'll open it."

I pulled the envelope flap out and then drew the card from the envelope and opened the card. I stared at the bill inside. "Ten dollars! It's only ten dollars!"

Without thinking I stared at my dad and then at my mom. "There was supposed to be a twenty-dollar bill in here."

My mom and dad broke out in laughter, especially Dad.

I stared at the ten-dollar bill, not comprehending.

"You didn't see me the other night watching you," Dad said.

"You saw me—?"

"You poked around and you opened that envelope."

I could only mutter a dejected, "Ten dollars."

It would be easy to say that from that night forward I learned not to open unsealed envelopes and not to poke around packages. But what I really learned was that my father could walk around the house with the stealth of Santa silently sliding down the chimney and watch me with knowing eyes.

It affected my life to this day, for I always assume that no matter what I am doing, no matter if I am alone—or seem to be alone—I should conduct myself in a way as if someone is watching me. And the truth is, God always watches me.

I also came to know I should be thankful for whatever I receive, because gifts come from the heart. My dad never gave me the other ten dollars. If he had, I probably would not have learned.

I don't even remember how I spent the ten dollars. I do remember the lesson I learned that Christmas.

36. Fighting at Christmas

Marcia Windness Coward

IN OUR SIXTH YEAR OF MARRIAGE, CHRISTMAS EVE WAS light-years from the cherished peace of our beloved hymn "Silent Night." My husband, Don, and I were at each other's throats rather than in each other's hearts as we attempted to put up our nine-foot spruce.

"No, not now!" I shrieked when Don let go of the tree that wobbled in its stand.

"Uh-oh!" Don shouted, and leaned to catch it. Too late, he landed on the floor and the tree was on top of him.

The excitement prompted our sixteen-month-old son, Thomas, to speak his first full sentence. "Da-da down!" he squealed.

That didn't amuse my husband, who was drenched in perspiration.

"Marcia, *please* get your son out of here," Don yelled, "before he gets smacked by an antique German Saint Nicholas!"

I grabbed Thomas.

My once-thoughtful husband had seemed to become more volatile with every wedding anniversary. He bickered. He pouted. He blew up. I knew he was under pressure at the orchestra, but our toddler could hardly understand his impatient, distracted father.

Why can't we live in harmony? I wondered many, many

times. *Will the seven-year itch apply to us?* My husband and I were older parents. He was forty-seven and I was three years younger. We had already been set in our ways before we were married. Don was a tall, thin cellist with piercing brown eyes and a receding hairline, and I was an events planner inclined to dressy suits and silk blouses.

After I put Thomas in his playpen, I helped Don set the tree upright and held it while he screwed it in place. "Good job, Don, now that you've pulled yourself up by your bootstraps."

"Shut up."

I shouldn't have said those words, but we were at war and fighting had become our normal way of life. We had engaged in so many heated arguments our tree was going up late.

We were on our own because Don's parents resided in assisted living in Florida and my father, a widower, lived in a nursing home in Arizona.

Just then, Thomas burst into tears. I pulled him from his playpen and occupied him with Bob the Builder construction toys. I thought Thomas lacked the hand-eye coordination to manage them, but Don had insisted his only son receive tools at age one. "Hammers, wrenches, and screwdrivers are essential to the male trade."

That had become the basis for another argument. "Have you forgotten your penchant for doing what you do best—performing and teaching—so you could pay people who know how to fix the dishwasher and seed the lawn?"

Studying the tree, we didn't notice Thomas leaving Builder Bob to open the door to our beagle's kennel. Boggles darted out, ran toward the tree, lifted a leg, and watered it.

Even little Thomas recognized something was wrong. "No, doggy down," he called out. Expecting play, Boggles jumped up and dislodged the tree from its stand.

The tree toppled again, knocking Thomas over. I picked him up and was unable to see any bruises, but he screamed and wouldn't stop.

When he wouldn't stop crying, Don dialed 911. Within minutes, we were in an ambulance careening around slushy street corners toward Hanover Hospital.

They gave Thomas a bed in the emergency department. After that they took him to Radiology. Don and I stared at the people who packed the waiting room—anguished victims of auto accidents as well as gun and knife attacks—and their grief-stricken loved ones.

Where is Christmas? I wondered. *When is Christmas?*

Don, staggered by the heartrending scene, moaned, "How far is it to Bethlehem?" (A traditional English carol.)

"Worlds away from here," I said.

Just then, Thomas returned in the arms of Dr. Jorge Corillo, an immigrant with a broad, swarthy face and black curls. "Except for a greenstick fracture of the right collarbone, Thomas is perfectly healthy," the doctor said. "His pain should subside in about two weeks. Of course, you'll need to keep him quiet to avoid further damage, and, since he's too young to express his distress clearly, you'll want to comfort him often."

I pressed for details.

"She always exacts more information," Don interrupted, "especially when everyone's out of words."

I kicked his shin.

Dr. Corillo put down his pen, paused, took Don's hand and mine, gripped them firmly, and placed mine in Don's. "Just to be safe, let's observe your son overnight," he suggested. "One of you can sleep in his room and the other in the lounge."

We both objected and insisted on being with Thomas on Christmas Eve. Dr. Corillo ordered two cots brought into Thomas's hospital room.

Pain medication lulled our toddler to sleep, still dressed in his red fleece jumpsuit and fringed hat. Until midnight, Don and I took turns patting our precious child's back, more to soothe ourselves than Thomas, whose steady breathing punctuated our stony silence.

After Thomas was asleep Don pulled me close. "We've been waiting for Christmas. Let's not let this one slip away," he whispered. "Christmas is not about trees; it's about loving. Christmas isn't about winning; it's about giving." He quoted the most familiar verse in the Bible: " 'For God so loved the world, that He gave His only begotten son . . .' Darling, we've forgotten the basics. Christmas is here, now, with the three of us. Santa Claus even sent us an elf!"

I smiled at Don's mixed metaphors—God and Santa watching out for us. But just then I realized how much I loved this good, insightful man.

From midnight on, Don and I shared one cot. I have never felt more married to my husband than I did that snowy winter night, as we clung to each other in need and want, grateful for life and love.

Thomas awoke his sweet, cheery self. Jorge Corillo came in to check on Thomas's condition. Missing his family in Guadalajara, Jorge invited us to eat Christmas dinner with him at a Mexican restaurant.

"Their burritos? Fantastic!" Jorge welcomed us in a faded sombrero and presented one to Thomas. After enjoying his burrito, Thomas stopped playing with his special hat so he could hold his fried ice cream—spoonfuls of which melted down his green velvet jacket. Resembling a woodland gnome with a sweet tooth, he responded to the doctor's kind touch by sitting on his lap throughout most of the meal. Jorge admitted, tearfully, that Thomas's presence helped make up for the absence of his own two-year-old, Antonio.

✳ ✳ ✳

The collarbone healed slowly. Whenever Thomas lifted his arm too far, he'd shout, "Down, down!"

That was our cue to hug him and respond, "You're right, Thomas; keep it down. But you're healing, lucky boy!"

Our blue spruce tree never returned to its living room corner. We declined buying a Christmas tree for several years. Our marriage counselor wisely believed that the lack of a tree would remind Don and me to negotiate minor issues and focus on the essentials during the often-stressful holiday seasons. Since then, we've gotten much better.

The following year, on October 12, Thomas gained an eight-pound sister. Our extroverted blue-eyed redhead was especially enchanted with our playful beagle, who'd become gentler with age. Thomas and Boggles were as thrilled with our new addition as were Don and I.

Observers joked about our timing: "Look what you discovered!

Do you call her Christa? Christine?" They referred to Christopher Columbus, who shares our daughter's birthday. That was as close as they came to a much different fact.

Don and I named our baby Cori, the treasured gift of our most dearly loved Christmas ever. She constantly reminds us of that stormy Christmas when we gathered together and makes us thankful that we came out wiser and happier.

37. With the Help of Friends

Jane McBride Choate

EARLY SATURDAY MORNING, DECEMBER 23, DOROTHY, MY eighty-two-year-old friend, phoned us. "Can you and Larry take me to the store?" she asked. "I want to pick up a few things before my company arrives."

"We'll be there in fifteen minutes," I promised.

Although she suffered from many physical ailments, Dorothy maintained a spirit of laughter and fun that infected everyone fortunate enough to call her friend.

Despite the nearly thirty years of age that separated us, we had become friends. I drove her to doctor appointments, to the store, to lunch at a small diner where she insisted on treating me. All the while, she encouraged me not to "drive like an old lady."

"I like to move," she said.

With a prayer on my lips and Dorothy's hand on my elbow, urging me to go faster, I speeded up.

One of Dorothy's favorite activities during the Christmas season was to go to a novelty store where we pushed the buttons of holiday characters, sending them into frenzied song and dance. No plush Santa, stuffed snowman, or gaily dressed elf was safe from our mischievous fingers. Clerks and shoppers gave us indulgent looks.

Dorothy walked with a pronounced slump, due to several

operations on her back and hips. Occasionally she used a cane, but she normally used a walker to get around. That December morning, while I waited in line with her at the store pharmacy for her prescriptions, she looked wistfully at a lightweight walker.

"I wish I had the money for that. It's the Cadillac of walkers." Like many seniors, Dorothy lived on a meager Social Security check that left little for extras.

No child wishing for a shiny red bike had ever gazed at wheels with such longing. Dorothy's old walker had to be lifted with every step. I checked the price of the walker and winced when I read it. It was more than our anemic checking account held.

My husband and I took Dorothy back to her apartment, helped her inside with her sack of groceries, and promised to visit the following day, Christmas Eve.

On the way home, an idea niggled at the back of my mind. Could we pull it off? Tentatively, I voiced it aloud to my husband. Could we buy the walker for Dorothy? Alone we couldn't afford it, but with the help of friends we could.

Only one problem remained: overcoming my embarrassment at admitting that we didn't have the money ourselves. I decided that pride wasn't as important as helping a friend. I e-mailed and called Dorothy's friends in the community and in our church, explained the situation, and stressed that any amount would help. The money began arriving. Five dollars here, ten dollars there.

With what my husband and I could contribute, we had enough to buy the walker, so we bought it. I also bought a card and took it to her friends to sign.

Christmas Eve fell on a Sunday. After the church service, my husband and I drove to Dorothy's home. She was with her brother and his wife and their two grown sons.

My husband carried in a large box topped with a bright green bow. "Merry Christmas," he said.

"You've already given me a present," Dorothy said.

"This is from all your friends." I said, and handed her the card containing more than a dozen signatures.

She repeated every name, still not understanding.

While she did that, Larry opened the box, pulled out the walker, and put it together.

The surprise and pleasure on Dorothy's face shone brightly. "You did this for me?"

"*We* did it," I said, gesturing to the card.

Dorothy used the walker constantly, becoming very adept at maneuvering it through grocery store aisles, at church, and at doctor appointments.

That wasn't the end of the story, though. The following year, Dorothy was again expecting her out-of-town relatives for the holidays. She wanted to be able to entertain them with a special meal, but she didn't have the money.

That need came out one day while we talked casually. A second time, I shelved my pride. I e-mailed and called friends. Again Dorothy's friends responded with generosity, despite a downturn in the economy. With the three hundred dollars we received, we bought a gift certificate at the grocery store, slipped it inside a card, and presented it to her a week before her relatives were due to arrive.

Tears gathered in her eyes. "It's too much. It's too much."

"It's exactly right," I said. "Exactly right for a special friend."

We took Dorothy shopping and encouraged her to splurge on a few delicacies as well as the essentials for Christmas dinner. Chocolates and cherries. Crab cakes and pasta salad. Sparkling apple juice and eggnog. She laughed delightedly over every extravagance, pressed my hand, and laughed again.

After the holidays, she called with stories of her family's pleasure in the unexpected feast.

It saddened me that Dorothy passed away six months later. At the funeral service held in our church, her brother spoke and thanked members of the congregation for caring so tenderly for his sister. Among other things, he recounted the Christmas gift.

I looked around at the faces of those attending and saw the same individuals and families who had contributed so freely to gifts for our dear friend.

Dorothy's spirit lives on, and I imagine her in heaven laughing at a joke and reminding me not to "drive like an old lady." I say a prayer and careen down the street, hoping Dorothy is proud of me.

38. An Irish Pub in Korea

Pamila Jo Florea

I'D ALWAYS WANTED TO TRAVEL, AND I HAD MY CHANCE when I took a job in South Korea. Teaching executives at their places of business opened up a new world of experiences for me—of adventure in an exotic setting. I hadn't anticipated that South Korea would be so beautiful. There was one problem for me—I spent most of my working hours driving from place to place. That provided no time for me to pause and chat with other teachers. All my students were men, so it would be improper in South Korea for them to become my friends. I didn't meet any women.

My only option was the Irish Pub, where the expatriates gathered most nights to drink, play poker, and shoot pool. I'm the daughter of an alcoholic, so I didn't like that option and I didn't want to be in such an atmosphere. Some of my most vivid memories of childhood involve the smell of my father's breath and his cruelty while he was drunk. Those painful memories kept me from any place that served alcohol.

As the months in Asia went by, I got on the Internet more often. I wrote on message boards, joined a chat room, and started a blog. I was desperate for English contact, and the Internet became my lifeline to the English-speaking world. Eventually I met many of those people, visited them, attended their weddings, even dated a few of the men. But that came later.

It was my first year in Korea and my first Christmas away from home. I was alone. I had no friends—no one to hug, no one for whom I could cook or who could accompany me to the movies. When I hiked, I walked the trails alone. I ate alone and did everything by myself.

My spirit dragged, and I counted the days until my contract expired and I could leave.

And now Christmas was almost here and, for the first time in my life, I dreaded the holiday season. I tried to make up for the aloneness by talking to my online friends, my sisters, and my friends back home. Most of them encouraged me to find something to do.

"You can't be alone on Christmas," they said. They meant well, but they had no idea how isolated I was. They also couldn't tell me what to do—only that I needed to do *something*.

A few days before Christmas, I opened the paper, clicked on a few Web sites, and scoured the bulletin boards on buses and restaurants. I read of events in far away Seoul and holiday gatherings in the nearby city of Busan but nothing in my little town. At last I found an ad for my little town that read: "Traditional Christmas Dinner."

That excited me until I read a little further and saw these words: "Come to the Irish Pub."

In desperation and after a full day of indecision, I decided that my loneliness was bigger than my apprehension. Besides, I had promised family and friends that I would do something. I picked up American candies I'd bought in the airport a few months earlier and started out for the pub. I figured I'd sit and eat chocolate-covered macadamia nuts if the evening turned out to be a bust.

The click of my cowboy boots against wet pavement was the

only sound I was aware of between my apartment building and the pub. Then the pub was right in front of me—a nondescript building on a nondescript street. I was delighted to see no drunken revelry going on outside

My breath steamed up the window as I peered inside. What I saw amazed me. The room was covered in banners. Poinsettias were everywhere and the pool table was the buffet table. The bar held a punch bowl filled with eggnog next to a stack of glasses.

Timidly I walked inside. From the speakers Gene Autry's voice sang "Rudolph the Red-nosed Reindeer."

Just then a pretty redheaded woman came up to me. "We wondered when you would finally come and hang with us."

I blinked back tears and squeezed her quick. She introduced herself, showed me around, and introduced me to a slew of familiar faces. I met an American who was taking magic lessons in exchange for teaching English classes; I spoke to a woman I regularly noticed at the spa. I shook hands with the teacher who waved to me when we frequently passed each other. Another man there taught Korean to the expats. I chatted with the woman with whom I had ridden to school during my first days in the city.

As I talked and laughed with the others, I realized I wasn't the only one lonely for home. The barkeep had learned about Western customs and opened the pub space for anyone who needed somewhere to go on Christmas Day.

Before long we sang Christmas carols and yuletide tunes. We shared our yams and squirted whipped-cream smiley faces on the pumpkin pies. Someone offered to pray. We reached around the table to hold hands. I assumed we all remembered our families back home. I know I did as I listened to him pray.

"Amen," we said, and when I looked up I realized I wasn't the only one with tears in my eyes.

I felt ashamed as I thought, *These expats have been here the whole time, open to me, but I've ignored them.*

No one seemed to notice that I was new. Instantly I became one of the group. People I didn't really know hugged me, and it was all right. I gave a number of hugs myself.

As evening turned to night, we finished eating and cleaning up, and I left after a quiet and sincere good-bye to everyone.

Back in my one-room apartment with my cell phone full of numbers, my stomach filled with mashed potatoes and turkey, and my calendar full of plans for the next few weeks, I lay on my bed and fell asleep. It was the soundest I had slept since I arrived in Korea.

Since then I've settled in Korea and become much more comfortable. But if it had not been for that year of loneliness, I would never have learned that Christmas is more than just songs, three-bean salad, or gifts under a tree. Christmas is the gathering of family, however we decide to define family.

Being far from home reminded me that all of us want to be loved—need to be loved—and we all need to belong. That year, my first in Korea, I was blessed to find that loneliness didn't have to keep me alone. I also learned that while bars still aren't for me, all celebrations don't have to take place in a house, a church, or a hall. Sometimes it's where two or three people are gathered together—even if the building is a bar. The attitude—the spirit— makes the difference.

39. All I Need

Liz Ballard

FLASHING RED LIGHTS RECEDED INTO THE DARKNESS AS THE ambulance drove away. My husband was inside and it was about four thirty on Sunday morning before Thanksgiving.

As I watched the vehicle disappear, I kept hearing the words inside my head: *Your life will never be the same.*

Perhaps that's obvious, but the change was even greater than I expected. Hours later, I learned the details of our financial collapse—something he had kept hidden from me. That's what had driven him to attempt suicide.

Later that day, I tried to face the reality of my position. My husband's wallet contained eleven dollars, our bank account was overdrawn, the gas tank registered nearly empty, and there was little food in the house.

My children and I made it through that week by powerful demonstrations of God's love, expressed to us by gifts of cash and bags of groceries from family and friends.

Twice-daily trips to the hospital, caring for our children, and worrying about the future wore me out. We spent Thanksgiving Day with my brother's family. They spread out a bountiful feast and I tried to be cheerful, but my emotional exhaustion prevented me from celebrating the start of the holiday season.

In our old lifestyle, I would have been taking out Christmas decorations and putting up the tree over Thanksgiving weekend. Now in preparation for my husband's return home I cleared out the medicine cabinet and kitchen cutlery (as directed by our counselor).

Despite all the bad things, I was able to thank God for intervening and sparing my husband. Now we had to rebuild our lives. But that wasn't foremost on my heart. Right then I had to focus on the more pressing issues involved in his release from the hospital.

A blur of activity consumed the weeks that followed, but not in the usual beginning-of-December ways. I would have been shopping for gifts, sending out cards, and making to-do lists. Instead, I interviewed for jobs and calculated how much debt we owed and how much we could pay on overdue bills. I spent hours on the phone trying to find emergency financial assistance. It seemed as if every call ended the same way: "All our resources have been depleted until after the first of the year."

As Christmas approached, things like presents and parties didn't cross my mind because of greater concerns: How would my teenage daughter deal with the trauma she'd experienced? Could we adjust to our two older sons moving back home? At least for a time after their father returned, I needed their help with his care and the running of our household. But having them back also meant a greater financial need, at least in the form of higher electric and grocery bills. Could they find new jobs? How would we pay the bills?

I don't know if I can even describe how it happened. We had absolutely nothing, yet somehow we made it from one day to the next. And we kept on making it. The electric power remained on. We didn't receive an eviction notice from our landlord, and the pantry shelves never emptied. Even more, nonessential things such as our Internet and cell-phone service continued without interruption. Every time we had a need, someone provided for us—and we didn't have to ask.

To be in the position where our survival depended on receiving from others humbled me. At the same time, the love poured out to us overwhelmed me. Our church paid our rent for two months as well as the large past-due electric bill. People sent gift cards for grocery stores and paid our phone bill. A dear friend gave me a stress-free day by taking me to lunch so I could get away for a while. Before she took me home, she bought take-out fried chicken so I wouldn't have to cook that evening. My sister sent a prepaid debit card with instructions that I should get my hair cut and buy needed personal items such as makeup.

We did nothing to deserve any of the gifts and had nothing to give in return. Yet because they loved us they gave anyway.

That year, we didn't exchange Christmas gifts. We finally put up an artificial tree and the decorations, and I did some of the usual baking in an attempt to make our home feel festive. None of us missed what we didn't have. We were enormously grateful for what we had already been given—a husband and dad, and a second chance together.

Relatives who lived in our area went out of town, so the five of us spent a quiet holiday at home. I planned to make our traditional ham dinner on Christmas Eve before we went to the candlelight service at church. However, I misjudged the time it would take to prepare and realized at the last minute I couldn't get everything ready in time. I ended up making a stir-fry dish. We laughed while we ate, because it reminded us of one of our favorite movies, *A Christmas Story*, where Ralphie and his family dine at a Chinese restaurant for their Christmas meal.

But the most poignant moment for me was when I sensed God's presence during the Christmas service. Just being together in the darkened church sanctuary with people we loved and who loved us, hearing the familiar songs and Scriptures, soothed my soul.

At the close of the service, musicians played "Carol of the Bells" while a poem scrolled across the video screen. The last three words hit me with a force I didn't expect. "Look up. Look up. It's time. It's time. God. With. Us."

God with us. I kept thinking of those three words.

That Christmas I didn't give any gifts, but I learned a profound truth. The advertising agencies and greeting card companies have it wrong. Christmas is not about giving. It's about *receiving.* "This is real love—not that we loved God, but that He loved us and sent His Son as a sacrifice to take away our sins" (1 John 4:10).

He came to us. God came *to me.*

What gift did I have to give Him? I was poor, wretched, and lost, not knowing where to turn or how to survive. And then God came. He came to bring the greatest gift the world could ever know. Salvation. Redemption. Love. For me. For my husband. For my family. I had done nothing and could do nothing and I had nothing to give in return. God gave it anyway, because He loves us.

My life has changed in many of the ways I expected, as I foresaw that November night; however, I couldn't have foreseen the changes that took place in my heart. Now I understand the elusive true meaning of Christmas. I've learned to receive God's love, in whatever form He gives it. And I've learned that's all I need.

40. Christmas in a Barn

Mary DeMuth

CHRISTMAS OF 2006, OUR FAMILY OF FIVE WAS HOMELESS. We didn't have any keys—not keys to a car and not keys to a home. We'd flown from southern France, leaving behind a ministry of more than two and a half years. We'd started small churches among the French and internationals near Nice; however, because of unrelenting stress and circumstances beyond our control, my husband, Patrick, and I decided to move back to the States with our three children, Sophie, Aidan, and Julia. Patrick and I came back discouraged and felt as if we had failed.

Before we returned we contacted friends and told them of our immediate needs. We needed a temporary place to stay—a place where we could bring our cat, Madeline. We had to have a place where we could stay long enough to locate schools, buy cars, and find permanent housing.

When we arrived at the Dallas airport, we had ten heavy suitcases of clothes and toiletries. The rest of our belongings would come across the Atlantic in a ship and then on to us by truck. Before we flew back to Texas, our close friend Leslie told me about mutual friends, Eddie and Sarah, who owned a camp. There was a sturdy barn, with a tiny apartment at one end. Outside were hundreds of acres of Texas pasture.

The apartment contained two small bedrooms, a kitchen, a

bathroom, and a living area. Life on the ranch slowed down in winter, and they seemed delighted to be able to help us.

We arrived at the Dallas airport six days before Christmas and I felt as if defeat clung to us. Dozens of friends waited for us in the international terminal with signs, hugs, laughter, and we shed a few tears. Another friend lent us a car. Warmed by an amazing welcome, we drove our borrowed car to the camp—a place we'd never been. We followed directions in the pitch-dark night, making plenty of wrong turns.

After we found Sabine Creek Ranch, we drove over the cattle guard toward what would become our home for a month. Our headlights brushed over a wide, open pasture that stood silent under a banner of stars. Horses stood behind electric fences. Strung white lights illuminated a small porch, a white plastic chair, a slab of concrete, a window, and a door in the corner of an aluminum-sided barn. We carried our large pieces of luggage into the apartment.

The place, usually unfurnished in the winter, had just the right number of beds, couches, and tables. Floor-to-ceiling food filled the pantry and the fridge. Friends had stocked the cabinets with dishes, cups, and cookware. One bedroom held three bunk beds, with a supply of linens, quilts, hangers, and a lamp.

In the other bedroom was a queen-sized bed along with two side tables with lamps. The heat had been turned on, which we appreciated because it was a cold night. We let our cat out of her metal cage and smiled because our friends had even provided a cat box and food.

Even more wonderful beyond that generosity, Christmas decorations gleamed in the small home. Our friends had obviously scrubbed the place before they decorated the living area. In the corner was a Christmas tree with presents underneath. Bandanas, spurs, and cowboy ornaments mingled with lights and ribbons. On the small dining table someone had left a plate of home-made Christmas cookies. Next to it we found mugs, cocoa, and marshmallows—everything needed for a cozy family evening.

Our family won't ever forget the moment love so tangibly blessed us. Patrick and I had so little and struggled with the sense of failure. But once we were inside and saw the bounteous provisions, we knew we were wonderfully loved. They couldn't have done more for us.

We invited another family to celebrate Christmas dinner with us. The children played outdoors, chased animals, and en-joyed the cool Texas winter. Inside Patrick and I unpacked and talked to our friends about France. Their presence encouraged us and their words and embraces alleviated our sense of failure.

Christmas felt appropriate in the corner of a barn. With no possessions, but rich in friends, we took a much-needed time to rest on the ranch. We went on walks, stared at the stars as if we hadn't seen them before. We took pictures, meandered through fields, and petted horses' velvet noses. We quietly listened to the soft sounds around us. We read books and watched movies on my husband's laptop—our only electronic form of entertainment. We woke to the mists that lingered along the brown-stubbled fields and we turned in as the sun gave up its fury with wildly orange skies.

Although we were warm, clothed, and loved, we understood more keenly the Savior's homelessness. He left the splendor of heaven for the sodden earth. We experienced barnyard life alongside Him, without much to call our own except our heavenly Father and our sweet family and friends.

Jesus was enough that Christmas. And as Patrick and I held hands and stared lovingly at each other, we knew—Jesus will always be enough. And it doesn't matter if we're in a house or a barn. He's still enough.

41. The Orange Post-it Note

Charles Stone

THREE YEARS INTO HEATHER'S REBELLION OUR STRUGGLES with her continued to mount. She had exhausted my patience. My anger teetered on the edge of rage. I wondered if I could possibly love her again.

I kept an office in the basement of our home where I studied before I went to the church office. One cold morning in December after another weekend of turmoil, I sat in my gray swivel chair in my office. I turned on my computer monitor and stuck a Christmas disc in the CD player. The instrumental music began to play through my tiny computer speakers as I studied.

"It's the Most Wonderful Time of the Year" was the first song, but I couldn't concentrate.

That's a bunch of bunk. Not for me this year. It's more like the worst time of the year. As the words came at me I mentally refuted them.

"Who has the right to tell me to be cheerful?" I said. "How can I be cheerful with a daughter like Heather?"

A few seconds later, the singer referred to Christmas as the happiest season. "I used to think so," I said to the singer on the CD. "Maybe if you don't have a teenage daughter bent on destroying your family."

The longer the music played, the worse I felt, especially when he sang about glowing hearts.

Glowing hearts? I buried my face in my hands. "Oh God, I'm ready to close my heart to her. The door barely remains ajar now. One more hurt from her and it shuts forever."

At least three times the soloist's and backup singers' voices blended as they told me it was the most wonderful time of the year.

"Enough of that music." I clicked to the next song. The next track began with quiet chirping of crickets and other nature sounds, followed by gentle ringing of Christmas bells. Then I heard: "Silent night, holy night, all is calm, all is bright . . ." Next the soothing sound of a mellow violin resonated with the cheerful sound of the bells and the warmth of background violins.

With no warning, I began to weep. Uncontrollable sobs racked my body as rivulets of tears flowed down my cheeks.

As I reflected on that majestic moment when divinity intersected humanity in the birth of Jesus, my emotions overwhelmed me.

These thoughts flooded my mind: *Lord, You came with an open heart You knew I would break. You knew I would reject and hurt You often. Yet Your love for me never wavered and You never closed Your heart to me. How can I close my heart to Heather? Who am I to reject her?*

Just then, someone walked down the stairs. I tried to wipe away my tears. The door opened. It was Heather. I turned my head away to hide my red eyes, but it was too late. Heather had already seen them.

She walked around my desk and stood behind me. She

wrapped her arms around my chest and laid her head on mine. Tears again flooded my eyes and they dripped onto her arms.

Then, with amazement, I felt warm drops of moisture on my head. Her tears of liquefied sorrow that fell on my head became soothing ointment to my wounded heart. As our two sorrows intermingled, I knew that my heart would always stay open to her.

I played "Silent Night" again to relish that holy moment. As the mellow violins finished the song, she unwrapped her arms from my chest and they glistened with tears.

She walked toward the door. I turned around, faced her, and said, "I love you, Heather."

The next day as I settled into my familiar gray swivel chair for another day's work, an orange Post-it note was on my computer monitor and I knew I hadn't put it there.

I leaned forward and read five simple words: "I love you, too, Dad."

Something mysterious and supernatural happened that morning. Where words had failed to communicate love, those tears that morning spoke with clarity. Although our troubles would continue and anger still surfaced, God had opened my heart to Heather, permanently. As we both felt each other's tears, a bonding began that God continues to build to this day.

Now, years later when I sit in that well-worn gray swivel chair, I see many smudged *I love you* Post-it notes that I've taped to my desk. They remind me of that moment when I learned to never close my heart to love.

42. Christmas Socks

Cam Flain

IN DECEMBER OF 1996, I STOPPED FOR A RED LIGHT WHILE driving to my office on Lower Wacker Drive in the Chicago Loop. It was about twenty-five degrees. A man was sleeping in a box on the sidewalk and his feet hung out. It wasn't the sight that most disturbed me. I was used to seeing homeless people, but he wore no shoes and no socks in the middle of winter. I wasn't used to seeing that.

I didn't stop, but the rest of the day I continued to think of that homeless man. The most obvious need was a sleeping bag. And not just for him but also for other homeless people to endure the cold northern winters.

That afternoon I got on the telephone and located a supplier who would give me a good discount if I bought several. I felt good that I could do something helpful. Before I bought them, I phoned the director of a homeless shelter and told him what I wanted to do.

"That's not really the answer," he said. "A sleeping bag will keep people warm, but we really want them to go to shelters, where we feed them, give them medical treatment, and provide counseling."

So making it more comfortable on the streets isn't the best way to help them, I said to myself after that call.

A few days later I spoke with a friend named Jack. We decided that we would buy a large number of heavy socks and take them to homeless shelters and they could distribute the socks on Christmas Eve. I already had family commitments for Christmas Eve, but Jack agreed to deliver the socks that he and I bought.

The next time we met, Jack beamed as he talked about what he did: "The people were so appreciative. They smiled, laughed, and a few hugged me."

We decided that for Christmas of 1997 we'd give even more socks to the needy. Both of us talked to people we knew and asked them to donate money. Most of them were glad to contribute. We decided to buy six-packs of tube socks. We encouraged our friends to buy two or three packs when they shopped with their families.

Before Christmas Eve, we had an enormous number of donated socks. The homeless shelters were usually in what I considered the dangerous section of Chicago, and I'd never been inside one. I reminded myself that I had a wife and two young children, it wasn't safe, and my wife didn't want me to go. That was only an excuse, but that's what I told Jack.

In 1998, we decided to do it again and had even more socks donated. We put up collection boxes in several office buildings, I spoke at churches; I did anything I could think of to get people to buy and donate socks. By Christmas Eve we had many, many thousands of socks. It was going to be a huge effort to distribute them.

"I'd really like you to go with me," Jack said. "It's too big a job for one person. With two of us we can both carry in socks and get done in much less time."

I was still too scared to go into those run-down, smelly housing developments and bad areas where murders happened regularly and crime was common. "Sorry, Jack," I said, "but I can't make it. You're on your own."

He stared at me a long time and I felt I was about the size of an insect. "It's okay, Tom, I understand."

Jack started to leave and I went from feeling incredibly uncomfortable to being overwhelmed with guilt. "I'll go with you," I said.

He smiled and I knew it was the right thing to do. I still didn't admit how fearful I was.

Early Christmas Eve morning, Jack came to pick me up with his cargo van. He had stopped at a local grocery store on the way to my house and bought three hams because they were on sale. "We can give them away randomly as we take in the socks."

"That's a great idea," I said.

We put the hams behind the driver's seat and loaded the van with boxes of socks and headed out. We went to dozens of shelters that day. At each shelter we dropped off a supply of socks and spent a little time with the clients and the children. We even played with some of the children.

To my surprise, it was a lot of fun, and although we did have a couple of scary moments, I enjoyed the experience. I also felt guilty for not having gone the previous years.

"One more shelter," Jack said, "and then we're done." He smiled in satisfaction.

I turned around to look into the back of the van. "The hams! We forgot to give out the hams," I said.

"We'll leave them at the last shelter. I haven't been there before," he said. "I think it's a small one, so if three hams are too many, I know a needy family who can use the extra one."

When we arrived at the last shelter, it was almost dark, very cold, and snowy and both of us were tired. Jack, who was driving, pulled up to the curb, jumped out, and ran around to the back to take out the last box of socks. I climbed in to get the hams.

As I was getting out of the back of the van a woman ran down the walkway. She was a nun and nearly bumped Jack off the sidewalk and stopped in front of me. "Do you have our meat?"

"What? I don't understand what—"

"Do you have my meat? Do you have *my meat*?" The second time was almost a shout.

"I don't know, but I've got these three hams." I showed them to her.

"Praise God you're here! Hurry up! Hurry up!" She turned and ran toward the house, praising God.

I had no idea what was going on and neither did Jack. He carried in the socks and I brought the three hams. We walked in through the open front door and faced a large dining room with a long table. It was decorated for Christmas dinner. I counted twenty-five settings.

"We have vegetables, potatoes, and dessert," the nun said. "We've been waiting for the meat."

Sensing my confusion, she explained that she and the other sisters had been praying for three days that someone would bring them meat for their Christmas dinner.

I stood, completely dumbfounded, holding three hams. As I handed her the hams, I calculated quickly. *Three,* I thought, *is the right amount of meat for twenty-five people.*

I lost track of the number of times they thanked us and praised God for us.

Jack and I drove home that night and we barely spoke as we absorbed what had just happened. God had worked a miracle that day to provide for twenty-five needy people. And God had used me in making that miracle happen.

I felt humbled and ashamed. I vowed to God that I would put myself in the place where He could use me to help others. And I've kept that promise.

Since Christmas of 1998, I've traveled in many different countries. One of my major projects is to provide clean drinking water to underdeveloped nations.

But the best memory I've ever had of helping others comes from that Christmas Eve when God answered the prayers of good people who reached out to Him.

And that is the Christmas spirit, isn't it? God reaches out to the needy and reminds them of His love.

Who We Are

Cheryl Barker lives in Coffeyville, Kansas. Her work appears in magazines, compilation books, on Blue Mountain Arts greeting cards, and in other publications. She is at work on her first book project. You will find her inspirational blog at www.cherylbarker.blogspot.com and may contact her at ckbarker@gmail.com.

Del Bates, a mother of three, lives in Vero Beach, Florida, with her husband, Jon. She delights in sharing the love of the Lord and encouraging others through writing, speaking, and facilitating a women's Bible study. Enjoy her many poems and devotionals by visiting her Web site at www.handstoblessu.com.

* * *

Twila Belk is a writer, speaker, radio personality, and director of two writers' conferences. She works full-time with bestselling author Cecil Murphey as his manager and personal assistant. For more information, visit www.gottatellsomebody.com.

Sylvia Bright-Green has published in ten anthologies and sold sixteen hundred articles to newspapers and national magazines during her thirty-five-year career. She has been president of local and state writers' associations, a talk-show host, and a college writing-marketing instructor.

Ada Brownell spent seventeen years as a daily newspaper reporter and has written for Christian publications since age sixteen. Her published work includes one book, more than two hundred articles and stories, and chapters in several books, including *50 Tough Questions* (Gospel Publishing House). Contact her at www.adabrownell.com or www.inkfromanearthenvessel.blogspot.com.

Patrick Burns is a professional photographer and paranormal investigator. Best known for his starring role on television's *Haunting Evidence*, he is also the co-author of *The Other Side: A Teen's Guide to Ghost Hunting and the Paranormal* (Houghton Mifflin Harcourt), written with Marley Gibson and Dave Schrader. Contact him at www.patrick-burns.com.

Jane McBride Choate is the author of thirty books for Harlequin, Kensington, and Avalon and more than two hundred short stories and articles. She considers writing to be the best job in the world.

Liz Collard is a writer and speaker living in Orlando, Florida, with her husband, Bob, and their children, Matthew, Jeremy, and McKenzie. She is the author of the *Building a Godly Marriage* series. Contact her at liz.collard@hotmail.com.

Marcia Windness Coward, writer, publicist, and photographer, has written hundreds of stories, newsletters, and journals for publication and nonprofit organizations in the Philadelphia area. U.S. 1 Worksheets, a poet's cooperative; *U.S. 1 Newspaper*; and the *Courier-Post* have published her poems. She teaches creative writing at Medford Arts Center. E-mail her at marcoward @comcast.net.

Mary DeMuth is an author and speaker who helps people turn their trials into triumphs. She has written ten books, including the Defiance, Texas, fiction trilogy (Zondervan) and a memoir, *Thin Places* (Zondervan). She lives with her family in Texas. Find out more about her at www.marydemuth.com.

Janet Perez Eckles, although blind, thrives as a Spanish interpreter, international speaker, writer, and author of *Trials of Today, Treasures for Tomorrow: Overcoming Adversities in Life* (Xulon Press). She enjoys working in church ministries and taking Caribbean cruises with her husband, Gene. Visit her at www .janetperezeckles.com.

Shawnelle Eliasen lives in Illinois. She and her husband, Lonny, rear their sons in a Victorian house near the Mississippi River. She has published in *Guideposts*, *Angels on Earth*, *Mom-Sense*, and *Marriage Partnership*, and several anthologies, including *Chicken Soup for the Soul* books, *Praying from the Heart*, *A Cup of Comfort for Couples*, and *Christmas Miracles*.

Sam Haim, P.E., is the chief executive officer of First Water Systems, Inc. (www.firstwaterinc.com), which develops advanced water purification technology for disaster relief and for underdeveloped countries. He is an author and speaker on these issues,

as well as on personal development. You can reach him at TomF
@FirstWaterInc.com.

Pamila Jo Florea is an ESL (English as a second language)
instructor in Korea. She feels lucky to get paid for what she loves
to do.

Ron Geelan is a full-time financial services professional and
part-time freelance writer. His essays and articles have appeared
in the *New Jersey Family* magazine, *Underwire*, *War Cry*, and *The
Dollar Stretcher*. You can reach him at rgeelan@optonline.net.

Marley Gibson is the author of the *Ghost Huntress* young
adult series and the co-author of *The Other Side: A Teen's Guide
to Ghost Hunting and the Paranormal* (Houghton Mifflin Harcourt), written with Patrick Burns and Dave Schrader. She also
has co-authored *Christmas Miracles* (St. Martin's Press) with
Cecil Murphey. She's a gourmet chef, certified SCUBA diver, and
avid traveler. Contact her at www.marleygibson.com or on Facebook at www.facebook.com/marley.h.gibson.

Linda Gilden is an experienced writer, speaker, editor, and
writing coach. An author and ghostwriter of many books and with
hundreds of magazine articles to her credit, Linda loves to share
a great story. Her greatest joy (and source of inspiration) is spending time with her family, especially at Christmas.

Susan Green, a wife, mother, and grandmother, is executive
director of Scenic City Women's Network, a ministry to work-

ing women in Chattanooga, Tennessee. She sees writing as one way to help people relate to God.

Chris Griffin served in the pastoral ministry for thirty-two years and is the founder of Newwine2go, a nonprofit speaking and writing ministry. You can read his weekly devotional, "Just a Thought," at www.newwine2go.com or follow him on Facebook at www.facebook.com/newwine2go.

Janet Morris Grimes, a wife and mother of three, has published her first book and is diligently working on her second. To follow her progress as a writer, visit her blog, Writing for the Pursuit of Sappiness, at www.janetmorrisgrimes.com.

JoAnn A. Grote has written more than thirty-five books, including adult and children's fiction and nonfiction for children. She is an award-winning author, and the Christian Booksellers Association bestseller lists have featured several of her titles. Reach her at jaghi@rconnect.com.

Jean Matthew Hall's stories have appeared in various magazines and anthologies including *The Embrace of a Father, Whispering in God's Ear, Chicken Soup for the Chocolate Lover's Soul, The Ultimate Gardener,* and *Christmas Miracles.* Contact her at www.jeanmatthewhall.blogspot.com.

Drienie Hattingh was born and raised in South Africa. She immigrated to the United States in 1986. Her columns and stories about life, love, and family have appeared in newspapers and magazines in California, Utah, Minnesota, and South Africa. She lives in Utah with her husband, Johan. Contact her at DrienieM @aol.com.

Nancy Haag is a wife, mother, grandmother, and author of a thousand articles, four books, and features in sixteen book compilations. Among her numerous awards are a 2008 Amy Award for "We Are the RV Care-A-Vanners," the story of her call to build Habitat for Humanity homes for deserving families.

Ruth Kaufman has had six of her manuscripts place in writing contests, including runner-up in Dorchester's *Romantic Times Book Reviews'* National American Title II Contest. An attorney with a master's degree in TV/radio, Ruth is an improv, on-camera, voice-over talent and a freelance editor. Visit her at www.ruthjkaufman.com or www.ruthtalks.com.

Woody McKay is a retired Presbyterian minister who has enjoyed writing and good humor for years. He shares his father's experiences when he worked for Henry Ford with many groups as well as Woody's own seventeen grandchildren. He has published several bits of his humor and Ford episodes.

Susan Miura is a book reviewer for FaithfulReader.com and author of "The Cotton Candy Man" in the *Missing* anthology. A former reporter, she now works for a library in public relations and also presents programs titled "A Taste of Italy" throughout the Chicago suburbs. Visit her "Takes the World" at www.susan -miura.blogspot.com.

Cecil Murphey has written or co-written more than one hundred books, including the *New York Times* bestseller *90 Minutes in Heaven* (Revell), written with Don Piper, and *Gifted Hand*s (Zondervan), written with Ben Carson. Cecil writes on a variety of subjects, including caregiving, aging, spiritual growth, and male sexual abuse. Contact him at www.cecilmurphey.com.

Terry Nelson with an English literature degree from Western Washington University, was a film critic for *The Chronicle* for more than a decade and wrote freelance news stories. He is currently finishing his novel, *Loonies in the Dugout.* Contact him at www.terrynelson.net or his Seattle Mariner blog: www.ball sandstrikes.mlblogs.com.

Susan Titus Osborn director of the Christian Communicator Manuscript Critique Service, has written or co-written thirty books; the latest is *Too Soon to Say Goodbye: Healing and Hope for Victims and Survivors of Suicide* (New Hope Publishers), written with Karen L. Kosmen and Jeenie Gordon. She lives in Fullerton, California, with her husband, Dick. Contact her at Susanosb@aol.com or www.christiancommunicator.com.

Jane Owen a retired teacher, has lived in seven states and served as a missionary in Haiti. She and her husband live in a cabin nestled in the West Virginia woods. Her articles have appeared in *CHERA Fellowship* and *Upper Room* and *In Touch* (online).

Dan Piper has been an ordained minister since 1985. Before that he was a radio and TV executive with CBS and CBN. He is an internationally recognized evangelist and co-author of four books, including *New York Times* bestseller *90 Minutes in Heaven* (Revell), written with Cecil Murphey. Visit Don at www .donpiperministries.com.

Brenda Poinsett shares life-changing knowledge and sparkling ideas through teaching, speaking, and writing. She's written fifteen books, including *The Friendship Factor: Why Women Need Other Women* (New Hope Publishers). Visit her at www .brendapoinsett.com.

Marty Prudhomme a freelance writer from Mandeville, Louisiana, has taught and written Bible studies and devotions for twenty-five years. She is the vice president of Leadership Training on the Louisiana State Board of Aglow International and serves as Outreach Coordinator for her local church.

Shirley Reynolds has published ninety stories from personal experiences, including articles on adoption, child abuse, and grandchildren, as well as devotions for adults and children. She loves to explore mountain trails, capture the beauty through photography, and share experiences by speaking at women's retreats. You can find her at heartprints@netzero.com.

Wayne Scheer has been nominated for four Pushcart Prizes and a Best of the Web award. His work has appeared in a variety of print and online publications. You can download *Revealing Moments*, a collection of twenty-four stories, at www.pearnoir. com/thumbscrews.htm or contact him at wvscheer@aol.com.

Viola Shimp retired after serving for many years as a Sunday school teacher for two- and three-year-olds.

Kelly J. Stigliano has been a speaker and writer for more than twenty years. She and her husband, Jerry, enjoy life in Orange Park, Florida. They have five children, a son-in-law, and a granddaughter. To learn more about Kelly, log onto www.kellys tigliano.com.

Charles Stone is a senior pastor and has served in vocational ministry thirty years. Dr. Stone has published twenty-five articles and two books. He writes on leadership and church ministry. His second book is *5 Ministry Killers and How to Defeat Them: Help for Frustrated Pastors* (Bethany House). Visit him online at www.charlesstone.net.

Annemarie B. Cait lives in Conshohocken, Pennsylvania, with her husband, Joe Beck, and Sammy, their Yorkie. Annemarie has contributed to several volumes of the *Chicken Soup* series, *Reminisce* magazine, and the Patchwork Path anthology series. She enjoys cooking as well as singing and recording American and Irish folk songs. You can reach her at irishbloom@aol.com.

Cindy Thomson is the author of *Celtic Wisdom: Treasures from Ireland* (Lion, UK) and a novel, *Brigid of Ireland* (Kregel Publications). She has published in several magazines, including *Clubhouse*, *True West*, and *Internet Genealogy*. She is a mentor with the Jerry B. Jenkins Christian Writers Guild. Visit her online at www.cindyswriting.com.

Lisa-Anne Wooldridge is an author, speaker, and teacher who makes her home in the San Francisco Bay Area with her husband, Andrew, and their three children, Jesse, Ivy, and Blaze. Contact Lisa-Anne at www.lisa-anne.net.

Lauren Yarger is the executive director of Masterwork Productions, Inc. As a member of Drama Desk and Outer Critics Circle she reviews Broadway and Off-Broadway shows at www .reflectionsinthelight.blogspot.com, which is the only source for a professional review with an added Christian perspective. Visit her writing blog at www.laurenyarger.wordpress.com.